Retailing Strategy

How to Do It!

Retailing Strategy

How to Do It!

by Richard J. Gentile

with Anne Gentile

Lebhar-Friedman Books
Chain Store Publishing Corp.
A Subsidiary of Lebhar-Friedman, Inc.
New York

For J. M. J.

Contents

Preface

The broad aim of this book is to give the reader a basic understanding of today's demand of consumer-oriented marketing and how tomorrow's long-range strategy, created at the top of the marketing plan, will make it tick.

The author's specific objective, however, is to demonstrate that strategy and effective retail advertising are within the grasp of any and all retailers, the Goliaths and the Davids. This book presents the idea that retail strategy problems are not individual novelties to be solved by a specialist, ad-hoc committee, or independent departmental action. Nor are the correct retailing solutions narrow or born of isolated concerns, but are instead formed and pushed forward by a new awareness of retailing's two connecting and life-sustaining necessities. From the beginning, at the top of the marketing plan, all of the retailer's goals, all of his strategies, all of the solutions to his problems, are fused together for pursuit of the two necessities. The strategist measures his investment productivity by these two necessities—cash flow and a near money target.

As you will see when you observe the many critical variables the retailer must stabilize, the strategic goals and implicit long-range strategies of advertising (developed and applied at the top of the marketing program) are part of a natural "good-of-total-store," overview promotional methodology.

It is at this point, at the top of the marketing plan, the strategist enters and "retailing strategy" begins.

Retailing Strategy presents first requirements first. To do otherwise would be a deliberate and grievous deception. I learned long ago about the importance of cash flow. Advertising layout, copy, and the greatest creative talents in the world will contribute little to the achievement of this aim if one's ship is not prepared for the voyage. Nor can an open mind be expected to hold the enterprise fast to a predetermined course. Nor can the mind be empty; there must be an input of some knowledge—some experience, our own and that of our ancestors. To begin anew would be to begin without a map of waters already charted. But, I have learned in my seminars, though the requirements for smooth and continued sailing may be clearcut to those among us who have had years of retailing experience, the disciplines and requirements of our business are not always immediately visible to the new enterpreneur. Oftentimes the teacher with much experience moves too quickly and, in no time at all, is quite distant from his inquisitive listeners. This book puts the propositions before you in a natural order, one leading to the other —toward one end—one postulate. The key that opens all doors is that there are two general types of strategy, *implicit*—created by headquarters or the master strategist, representing the long-range plan, and *intrinsic*—that deals with the local store, the short-range plan, the tactics for each specific promotional month. Intrinsic strategy is born of the first—implicit.

How this is done is what my book is all about.

—R. J. G.
Chicago
January, 1978

Acknowledgments

My thanks and gratitude go to the new entrepreneurs in my seminars for their questions, arguments, and eventual kind acknowledgment of retailing's truths; to an extraordinary man—Paul DeBacco —without whom this manuscript could not have been produced; to my author friend Bill Park for his kind help and encouragement of my work; to Barbara Miller, editor of Lebhar-Friedman Books, for keeping me on the right track; to the Federal Trade Commission for their excellent guides to honesty in advertising; and to authors Charles Tavel and Stafford Beer for their fine inspirational works which sparked the idea. I am indebted to all for their contribution to the statement that indeed, retailing is a science, and it is time we get on with it.

PART I
Implicit Strategy:
The Long-Range Tactical Plan

Trust thyself,
every heart vibrates
to that iron string.
—Ralph Waldo Emerson

1

CRISIS:

A Time to Choose

Why strategy?

This question is one a teacher would ask, not a businessman. A more potent and timely question for the entrepreneur would be—without strategy, who will you follow?

Before you answer the question, consider, if you will, this idea which is now generally popularized and, more often than not, acknowledged as fact: The important influence centers in our society are the super institutions, and they will gain still greater influence, power, and central control. None of us in today's society, we are told, as a group or as individuals, can exist and be free without depending on the large institution, providing, of course, the institutions remain in a responsible autonomy.

This may indeed be truth, but there is a flaw in the proposition that suggests further investigation.

Big institution influence, of course, was not always the case. In Peter Drucker's book, *Management,* he reminds us that ours at one time was a business society, and indeed, business was extremely powerful. More so than the institutions. But since the turn of the century, the importance and influence of business has decreased steadily.

Business of course has grown, but the institutions have grown faster. In his book, Drucker states that over 50 percent or perhaps as much as 60 percent of the GNP today does not go to the business section but to or through public service institutions. And though some people may still believe in our great industrial power, the truth is no one has the power that today's big universities have. In earlier times, no institution would ever have been allowed such power. Whether we like to hear it or not, Mr. Drucker's remarks are correct.

And in this new era of central management control and influence, an age of subsidies, however the writers, professors, government, and economists will identify and explain this particular period of time, the message is also clear; the conspicuous absence of reference to retailers in the volumes of management texts available shows that the retailer is not expected to play a significant or influential role. Our leaders tell us the major creative resources and innovations necessary for a new and healthy economy will come from the knowledge managers of the super institutions.

Creativity and innovation are, of course, two prime needs of our society, they always were. Whether they come from the large institution or the small independent enterprise, or both, is an unimportant conjecture. The real threat remains that, regardless of how small or large a retailer you are, retailers will be affected, for better or worse, by many outside decisions they did not make. To create effective strategy, we have to understand that our present age of retailing is indeed different from the '50s and '60s. We will have to take a world view of outside factors and, more important, the driving forces behind them. But there is another and greater threat, a question that deals with basic survival.

THE CRISIS

The rise of the institutions has taken place in a short period of time—the most dramatic increase being the space-age business boom of the past twenty years. In the same period, from the end of World War II to the end of the 1960s, professional management also experienced a world-wide boom. But the business boom ended; the fact that the end of the management boom coincided with the end of the economic boom may or may not be coincidental. The fact for you to consider is that, not unlike our own industry, the big institutions and professional managers are also in a questionable and unhealthy economic position. The daily newspapers tell us all is not going well for the institutions. Not unlike ourselves, what has been done has not been done all that well. One and all are struggling for their own basic survival.

The crisis then is that our immediate economic future is unknown. No one can give you a precise answer that will assure your safety. Your guess as to what creativity and innovations will work and where each will come from is as good as anyone's. Further evidence that individual enterprises will require a map instead of idle drifting can be found in the hard and obvious actuality that our economic and political systems are severely peppered with incompetence, greed, propaganda, and corruption.

In addition, we do not now and will not in the future have control over major political, social, or technological trends. We'll all simply have to accept them. To be able to adapt, we will, however, have to know what the trends are and where they will lead. You will have no choice but to outdo your competitors. Tomorrow's success will be in your own hands. Both Tavel and Drucker tell us this. You will either manage or you will mismanage. Perform or not perform. Succeed or fail. Lead or follow.

The new strategy objective therefore will not be one of maximizing profit, nor will it be an attempt to *minimize* risks. Your new objective is to *avoid crisis* in order to have the ability to *perform* your basic function of meeting customer demands and needs, when, where, at the price, and in the quantities the consumer dictates. The only meaningful yardstick of your productivity will be the daily receipts in your cash register. Very simply, the new age you are entering is recognized as a return to the individual, the *entrepreneur*. But today's entrepreneur will be different from the pioneer of yesterday.

THE NEW STRATEGY

Three essentials will characterize the new retailing age. First will be *overview*, not only of the inner workings of your company, but above all, of *the outside factors* that act upon your enterprise. Second, a company's management will be marked by the *personality* of its chief executive. He or she will be the unifying strategist, more an entrepreneur than an administrator. This is not new to our history, but the entrepreneur of this age will be of a new type. Third, strategy will be essentially *creative*. Original thinking will be required if a company is to outperform its competitors by *meeting the needs of the market* better than they do. This creativity will be in the hands of the generalist.

An overview of the outside factors which act upon your enterprise is not restricted to watching what your competitors and other retailing enterprises are doing. Every retailer should already be aware of his competition, not for the purpose of following suit, but for just knowing what is going on. The new overview will be aware of factors in your community that affect the environment, economically and physically, such as rezoning, dispersion of government and state dollars, the effect of subsidies in reducing consumer spendable income, and any specific subsidies that reduce your competitiveness. Inflation and dispersion of employment also affect the retailer's strategy decisions. Academic fund-raising takes millions in purchasing power out of a community. Whether this is wrong or right is not our concern in this book, but the fact that a pursuit of consumer dollars by non-business institutions is a reality, makes the new overview a necessity for the future.

The general message then is that a retailer can no longer drift with the current. In the absence of a boom economy, questions of personal survival are revived and the entrepreneurial personality returns. Our new entrepreneur will have a wide overview, an awareness of the outside factors, and most important, he will be:

- Creative
- An innovator
- A strategist

The emphasis will be on strategy, but this does not mean good management will be less imperative. Strategy *is* managing!

Our concern here will be:
1. Campaign planning—defining of long-range objectives
2. Directing—ways objectives will be achieved
3. Establishing priorities

Strategy then is a comprehensive view of the factors affecting your total performance. You must see the whole picture but not be too close to the nitty-gritty.

Tavel separates strategy into seven distinct types. All are adaptable to our industry:

1. **Financial**—securing dollars and investment
2. **Marketing**—stimulating sales
3. **Production**—locations, systems, and methods
4. **Geographical**—market
5. **Research**—reestablishment of programs
6. **Product**—long term production program (your store)

The combination of all six is the seventh strategy type. It is called:

7. **Global**

The correct promotional strategy choice for the retailer is "global."

The new creative managing task involving all strategies will not be an easy one, because old and unwanted boom economy managing philosophy's roots are always long and run deep into the system. Your future will depend upon an intellectual planning base, supported by fact, and cannot consist of bottom end marketing or last-minute open-endedness following whims or intuition. You will need a map. We, of course, are not striving to develop a reason for our being that does not already exist. Our industry is extremely important to our nation's economy and society's general health. We are a nation of shops and services: whether they be under one large roof or many single units is unimportant to the consumer. Though it is true the influence of business in the community has lessened in the past twenty years, whatever the reasons may be, nonetheless, the best economic dollar has got to be the one the retailer spends in local media, again, again, again, and again. And because I have had management responsibilities in two similar general merchandise stores (different companies), one highly creative—producing $200 per square foot of selling space and the other $54—I have to believe the economic dollar does not end with the retailer but, instead, begins there.

It is also becoming clear that the cause of business failure is not incompetence—which has been generally believed—but instead a lack of creativity, largely due to a boom economy that perpetuates only one strategy type—financial management for immediate results, a maximizing of profit and little or no innovation. It has also become evident a boom economy is detrimental to the true retail advertising function: During a boom period, under financial management, sales promotion is given precedence over advertising, production leads the retailer, and everyone and anyone sells everything and anything to everyone, any time, any place. We have to believe the time-consuming requirements of effective retail advertising are demands the financial-influenced retailer felt he could do without.

In a boom, the market is milked for its worth. The committee flourishes. Advertising and merchandising expertise, disciplines and responsibilities, are all declared antiquated. The computer is popularized and there is a massive diffusion of individual responsibilities and authority. The basics of retailing are forgotten in the immediate pursuit of sales. Short-range plans are "in"; long-range plans are "out". Businesses under financial-centered management keep growing, expanding, and merging, but only physically, not by increasing sales per square foot of selling space. Everyone does his own thing. Many retailing concepts are promoted that often are really acts of desperation.

This short-range promotion approach, which is subject to operating and financial influences, will generally hold its popularity as long as the boom economy exists. In a depressed economy, however, this retailing approach would be suicidal.

If we can agree that our retailing crisis is indeed real and the exclusive financial strategies that worked yesterday will not work today, then we will also agree that the solution has got to be found this week or within a short time thereafter. But the knowledge and experience we may gain in a week or two will contribute little to our immediate safety; we need "right now" improvements for our general well-being.

The task of hurriedly gaining insight to the wherefores of managing a multitude of subsystems that exist in a retail business is indeed a job one can hardly complete in one week. But, if you choose to bring your days of drifting to a quick end, there is a trick that can be used.

The trick, Beer suggests,[1] is to start with a modestly sized

---

[1] Stafford Beer, *Management Science* (New York: Doubleday & Co., 1967).

FIGURE 1.
Modestly sized model of simple resolution.

To understand the total system, start from the top of the model and descend. As you descend, the task gets bigger and bigger.

1—Strategist overview
2—Raw source factors
3—Sources of supply
4—Buying promotional goods and replenishing basics
5—Shipping and receiving

6—Marking, storing, accounting, ordering, adjustments and paying, payroll, advertising charges
7—Counting, display, advertising, personal selling
A—Cash flow

model. The model for our industry has the strategist on top, and moving downward, the major divisions of the system greatly expand the model. By working downward slowly, one can learn what major systems of your retailing activity are of urgent importance and which are relatively unimportant.

The task can become difficult, however, if you let yourself move into the nitty-gritty problems of retailing's subsystems, of which there are many. The interdependence and importance of the subsystems to the total cannot, of course, be easily dismissed. And we do not want to do so. But before subsystems can be fixed and interlocked, there must be an overview of the total system. We need *policy*, but before policy can be written, we have to know who we are, where we are going, why and how we will get there.

This can be done and is relatively simple: but the price is discipline! To have discipline, there must be policy. Both discipline and policy in turn will affect control. With discipline, policy, and control, you can then attain responsible decision-taking. And with discipline, policy, control, and responsible decision-taking, you will be able to manage strategically for good-of-total-store.

AN AGE OF DILEMMA

Many knowledgeable historians tell us there has been no other age comparable to ours. This I believe, and regardless of how it came about, our leaders also tell us we can do little about it. This has become evident to the most naive among us, but it does not mean you cannot do anything about your own personal survival and general well-being. To survive, in addition to managing your own business well, it appears obvious that you will have to develop an acute awareness of what is going on about you.

Consider the implications of this news item.

WASHINGTON (AP)—Sen. S. I. Hayakawa (R. Calif.) says the U.S. Civil Rights Commission is prying into "the private business of book publishing."

He and five other Republican senators cited a letter sent Aug. 17 by the commission to several textbook publishers saying it was "investigating the nature, extent, and impact of textbook biases." Hayakawa said the commission is asking publishers to submit the guidelines they give their authors to ensure their texts are not racist or sexist so that it may distribute a "resource list" throughout the country. "The publishers of America are meekly submitting to the commission their guidelines for producing officially approved books," he said. He predicted "further federal restrictions if textbook publishers do not defend their civil rights against the interference of the Civil Rights Commission."

The next step will be for the Department of Health, Education and Welfare to pressure schools to use only federally sanctioned textbooks. Otherwise, school districts will lose federal funds. It is only a matter of time.[2]

Senator Hayakawa's warning made me recall an incident that happened a decade ago. A director of a large, nonprofit, advertising policing agency told me he would welcome the day "sales" would be outlawed. The gentleman, of course, meant well, but by his comment, it was obvious he had little insight into what retail advertising is all about. There are many advertisers who lack integrity in their advertising approach, but honest "sales" are not in any form immoral and are in fact a necessary function of retailing. I could never come to believe this gentleman's wish would ever represent a serious threat. But when one reads Senator Hayakawa's warning, the possibility is indeed real. All the textbooks would have to do is denounce "sales," and outlaw them as detrimental to the health of our economy and the communities' general well-being.

And consider this article which appeared about the same time. This is another fine example of your need to be aware of what is going on about you.

WASHINGTON—At a hearing of the Securities and Exchange Commission, Joel Seligman, a brilliant, articulate, young law professor who is a member of a Ralph Nader consumer advocate group, pressed for legislation to require American corporations to have boards of directors divorced from management. Only in that fashion, he argued, can there be independent directors and true "shareholder democracy."

"The typical American corporation today," Seligman testified, "is directed by directors who do not direct."

To obtain independent directors who are not "financial gigolos," Seligman would bar officers of corporations, including the chief executive officer, from serving as directors, nominating candidates for directors and voting shares they own for directors.

Thus, in pursuit of corporate democracy, Seligman would dis-

---

[2] *The Kansas City Times*, October 14, 1977.

franchise those who, through their day-to-day work, presumably know most about company affairs. The formless body of shareholders, without the advice and consent of management, would be burdened with the responsibility of nominating and electing directors.

Irving M. Pollack, an SEC commissioner, raised this hypothetical question at the hearing: What occurs after an independent board of directors fires a chief executive officer and selects a successor? A change in relationships then takes place. The new chief executive officer is the creature of the independent board. As a result, independence diminishes. Perhaps it disappears. If the board that selected the chief executive officer found him wanting, it would, in effect, find itself wanting.

Thus did Pollack pierce the illusion of absolute independence.[3]

This article recalls what Charles Tavel reported in his book, *The Third Industrial Age—Strategy for Business Survival:*[4]

A new phenomenon, however, which is unknown in Japan and hardly known in the United States,[5] is emerging in Europe: The demand being made by the unions to introduce, through political channels, a legal right for employee representatives to participate in decision-making processes up to the highest levels. Unions in some countries like France, Italy, and Belgium, are reluctant to take such a step because, being Marxist oriented, they do not want to play the capitalist game. The German Social Democrat Party, on the other hand, demands equal representation of labor and management on the "Supervisory Boards" of both government-owned and private companies beyond a certain size. A law dating back to 1952 already provides for one-third representation of the employees on the Supervisory Boards of big corporations, except in the coal and steel industries, where equal representation has been in force since 1951. In Great Britain, the Labour Party goes still further. In June 1974, it published a "Green Paper" in which it advocates a reform of the corporation's legal structure which would result in strategy (long-term policy) being decided by a "Top Supervisory Board" on which the staff's representation would be at least 50 percent. This board would make all the important decisions and the management would carry them out. The immediate introduction of this reform is demanded

---

[3] J. A. Livingston in *The Kansas City Star*, October 12, 1977, p. 20A.
[4] Chapter 9, "Man the King," p. 225.
[5] Yet, the American unions may also begin to press for such participation, through collective bargaining at least.

for companies with more than 2,000 employees and later on for those with more than 200.

When you consider Tavel's remarks, you have to suspect Mr. Joel Seligman's Corporate Democracy plea is very real and we will hear more of it. And whether the idea is correct or wrong, history will tell us. The fact remains, however, censorship of texts and an authoritative "outside" Board of Directors will lead us to many highly questionable conditions.

You will have no control over these forces; you will have to adapt to them and to decisions made by others. But, remembering all has not gone and is not going well for the corporations, or the academic world, or the government, or labor, or individuals, it would seem most prudent for the new entrepreneur to place his reliance on his own judgment and ability to avoid crisis.

Sword of Common Sense!
Our surest gift.

—George Meredith

2

Managing the Business:

2 + 2 = 5

Our immediate task is to build a strategy model. But before this can be accomplished, you must clear your mind of any understanding you presently hold about retailing. Erase all the arguments, all trivia, the man-made concepts, all the old philosophies and the new, all the financial/operating management theories and futurology nonsense. What is left standing is the historic aim of any and every retailing enterprise—cash flow! And if we wipe our minds clean of all of the theories of how to achieve cash flow, the target still remains—near money!

The whole of promotional synergy[6] can be reduced down to a perpetual cash flow aim and a constant near money target. It is of these two retailing truths that strategy is born. Retailing strategy, very simply defined, is the strategic timing and placement of merchandise announcements (advertising) and inducements (sales promotion) to move the retailer's *total* inventory to and through the

---

[6] The word synergy describes a process of combining several oprations in such a way that the total result is greater than the sum of all acting independently. A common abbreviated definition is 2 + 2 = 5.

retailer's store *within the timetable limitations of traditional retail selling opportunities.* The desired result is cash flow, a feat considerably more complex than a "let's run an ad" intuitive decision.

Strategy, then, is a "good-of-total-store" proposition. Contrary to popular opinion, advertising is not the cause of success, but instead only aids success and will do so dramatically if it is programmed at the top of the retailer's marketing plan. And herein lies a problem. Few know how to focus on the challenge.

The key that opens all doors to successful advertising management and full productivity is the recognition and understanding that retailing is a two-dimensional managing enterprise.

There are two distinct management tasks to the business of retailing, each with its own disciplines, its own policies, its own decision-taking (choice), and its own controls and strategy. The first and largest task is the general business of retailing: the initial determination of goods the store will carry (representative of anticipated consumer needs), the stocking and display of the goods, and their eventual replenishment for day-to-day selling. This segment represents the retailer's basic inventory or service, the "good thing," the retailer's reason for being. This general business segment will account for some 70 or 80 percent of total sales.

The second task of the retailer's business activity is what this book is all about—the promotional, the broad merchandising strategies for the purpose of quickly moving the retailer's general inventory to and through the store. To accomplish this, some 15 to 20 percent of the retailer's inventory will be offered and sold to consumers at reduced or special prices. *This 20 percent sales volume in promotional goods is not left to chance but instead strategically programmed.* The advertising strategy is not overly concerned with selling the advertised items exclusively, nor with long durations or large quantities, but instead assures that potential customers visit the retailer's store first, and at the retailer's strategic times. The retailer's key selling time is usually marked by a designated event corresponding to the timetable of traditional retail selling opportunities.

At this point, a very important distinction can be made between the two parts of the retail business. Both are intellectual managing tasks. The first is largely financial, operating, and distributive; a buying, personal selling, and stock replenishment function. The

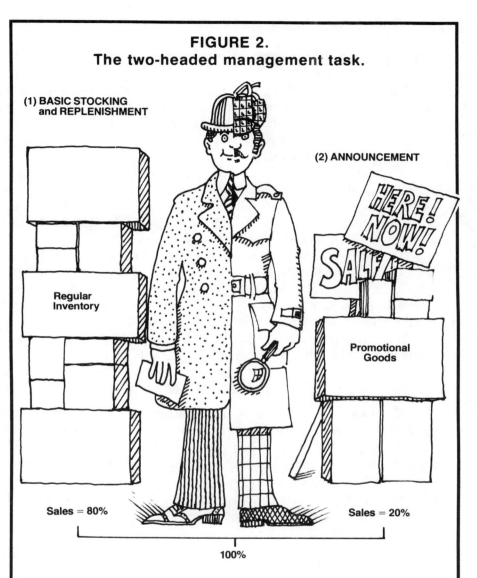

FIGURE 2.
The two-headed management task.

(1) BASIC STOCKING and REPLENISHMENT

(2) ANNOUNCEMENT

Regular Inventory

HERE! NOW!

SALE

Promotional Goods

Sales = 80%

Sales = 20%

100%

Note that the personality of the retailer changes from business manager to master sleuth. To gain satisfactory turns—the movement of total inventory to and through the store—you must dig for clues that lead to that success.

Successful strategy is the result of playing known "winners" (items) and of improving "sleeper" lines and/or items. You have to find the "winners" and the "sleepers" by investigating the performance in the first segment. And a good strategist holds all departments suspect.

second part is a clear-cut promotional function of merchandising and advertising strategies.

Though the second segment may only produce some 20 percent of total sales, its aim is to affect the *total store* sales. Because of this aim, *to effect total*, the strategist's task is a complex one of policy, decision-taking, and control which, to be successful, must begin at the top of the marketing plan.

To gain further insight into the immense scope and seriousness of the managing task for the second segment, review Figure 3. Pinpoint on the chart the spot where your advertising activity begins. For many retailers, it is the fourth box up from the bottom, to the right of the illustration's center. The ad schedule!

The realization that you are engaging in bottom-end marketing should cause some alarm when you consider how much of the true advertising role you are missing. Figure 3 is an illustration of the advertising function and its mainstream influence which is common to all retailing endeavors, regardless of their type or size.

When one reviews the chart, it is easy to understand why many retailers consider advertising a necessary evil.

THE SOLUTION

Effective strategy requires that the two business segments be separated into two distinct managing tasks. From a managing control and policy point of view, when the buyer functions in the second segment, he or she should not think as a buyer, but instead as a merchandiser, following the strategist's lead for *good-of-total-store*. Each segment has its own intellectual task of policy, decision-taking, and control.

1. *The general business.* The first and most important segment, your reason for being, representing some 80% of total sales.

2. *The promotional.* The second segment, to effect movement of total inventory, representing some 20% of total sales.

If you can agree to separate the two segments, from a managing point of view, you will begin to see how the complex strategy problem will be resolved. The point missed by many retailers is that both segments require strategy, and each requires the seven types men-

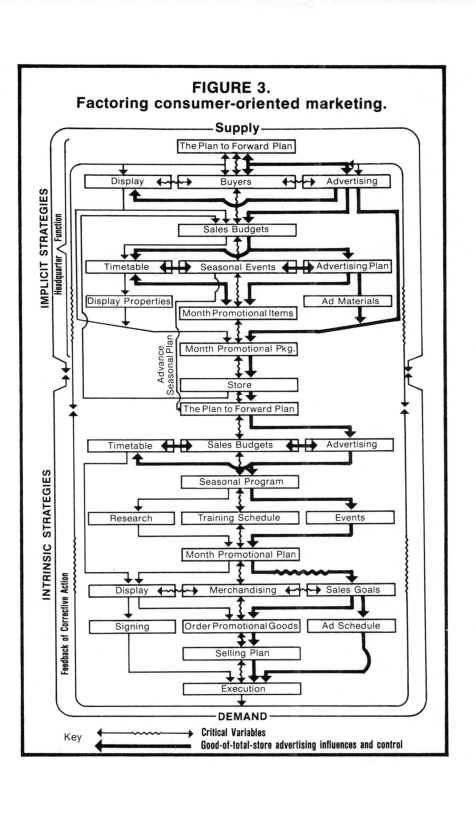

FIGURE 3.
Factoring consumer-oriented marketing.

Supply

The Plan to Forward Plan

| Display | Buyers | Advertising |

Sales Budgets

| Timetable | Seasonal Events | Advertising Plan |

| Display Properties | | Ad Materials |

Month Promotional Items

Month Promotional Pkg.

Store

The Plan to Forward Plan

| Timetable | Sales Budgets | Advertising |

Seasonal Program

| Research | Training Schedule | Events |

Month Promotional Plan

| Display | Merchandising | Sales Goals |

| Signing | Order Promotional Goods | Ad Schedule |

Selling Plan

Execution

DEMAND

IMPLICIT STRATEGIES

Headquarter Function

INTRINSIC STRATEGIES

Advance Seasonal Plan

Feedback of Corrective Action

Key — Critical Variables

Good-of-total-store advertising influences and control

tioned in Chapter 1, but for each segment the strategies are different in content and schedule.

The following example of the variance of time periods for the two segments should be sufficient to support the proposition for two distinct managing tasks.

TABLE 2-1.
Example of variance of time period for two segments.

FIRST SEGMENT		STRATEGY	SECOND SEGMENT	
Long Range	Short Range		Long Range	Short Range
10 years	3 years	FINANCIAL	1 year	6 months
5 years	2 years	MARKETING	6 months	1 month
7 years	3 years	PRODUCTION	1 year	6 months
20 years	10 years	GEOGRAPHICAL	1 year	6 months
10 years	3 years	RESEARCH	6 months	1 month
20 years	10 years	PRODUCT	1 year	6 months
20 years	10 years	GLOBAL	1 year	6 months

The time periods I specified are examples,—only you can determine the correct time periods for each segment of your specific business. My purpose is to show that there are indeed different requirements for each segment. Each one needs strategy, but not the same strategy nor for the same length of time.

There is one more strategy point, at least for the second segment of the business, the part our book and model are concerned with—marketing.

There are, as noted, two kinds of marketing strategy, the long range and the short. Throughout this book, the long-range strategy plan is referred to as implicit strategy. It is the headquarters or chief executive plan. It is primarily a tool of policy and control. The second, the short range, is identified as intrinsic strategy; it is born of the first and may also be identified with the stratagems and tactics used. It is, however, largely concerned with decision-taking. For a chain, implicit strategy is the headquarters' function, intrinsic is the local store's. If yours is a one-person enterprise, you'll be planning implicitly when you think like the president who is concerned about the total good of store for an approaching season, and implicitly when you wear the hat of the store manager facing the coming month. The small retailer's "implicit" strategy may be written down on a single sheet of legal-size paper under the heading "first six months' strategy." In a large corporation, "implicit" strategy might fill several 100-page volumes covering the six-month promotional period. Both efforts are strategy planning.

The argument presented here is that the promotional segment of the business is distinct for all retailers and must be separated intellectually and functionally from the general business of retailing regardless of the store size or type.

The benefits will be many.

THE NEED FOR POLICY

Establishment of policy is necessary to assure that what you are, who you are, and your reason for being are adhered to. If policy is clearly presented by top management, your business will not erratically evolve into something you never intended it to be. If yours is a hardware store, you must determine where your merchandise assortments will end, the type of goods you will carry, whether or not you will ever carry "seconds", what your item basics will be and how you expect to see a 100 percent in-stock condition on those basics, and so on.

You should have coverage policy for the development, buying, and receiving of seasonal goods. A source of supply policy is also required. There are many more needs for policy, but the basic and most important are:

- Advertising
- Display and signing
- Merchandising
- Merchandise coverage (seasonals and basics)
- Promotional markdown
- Promotional merchandising
- Old merchandise liquidation
- Sources of supply
- Pricing

Adherence to a policy for these major areas allows strategy to work. With policy—quite naturally—you create your store's image. The image the consumer receives of your store is not created by what you say, regardless of how many times you may say it, but instead by what you do and what the customer sees. If you say yours is a hardware store and you carry large assortments of gift items, housewares, electronics, and major electrical appliances, the consumer will not say, "Now that's a hardware store." People will not know what to call you. If you have serious out-of-stocks on basics, the consumer will begin to believe you are a "onesy-twosy" store, a special-purchase or outlet operation. If you have no strong seasonal coverages of key merchandise, goods a consumer can rightfully expect in your type of store, the image you have of your own store and the image the consumer will have will be quite different.

If you have no merchandise policy, the consumer cannot form an image of who or what you are.

One of the best general merchandise policies, and the simplest from an investment and dynamic promotional point of view, is used by the most successful retailer in the world and is known and understood by millions of consumers. But few retailers follow this company's lead.

Some fifty years ago, to avoid the dictates of manufacturers who would not cooperate in systems and methods to lower costs, Sears began to create its own private labels. This led to a merchandise and pricing policy. To this day, it avoids excessive assortments without reducing its full market potential. Sears' basic merchandising policy[7] is a consistent presentation of:

- Good
- Better
- Best

And by no accident, the bulk of its sales over the decades has been in the better category. The message for you is that whatever your business is, whatever you wish it to be, you must have policy to promote adherence to your wishes. Your wishes, what your store is,

---

[7] Boris Emmet and John E. Jeuck, *Catalogues and Counters* (Illinois: University of Chicago Press, 1950).

will become your image. But just as important—for our purpose—policy is necessary to make strategy a workable function.

Efficiency and discipline must be established and retained. However it should also be kept in mind that people (employees) must be allowed to express themselves and exercise initiative. The retailer's main reliance will always be on men and women. Their self-reliance and initiative must always be protected and any elaborate policy checks or systems will, of course, destroy it. But initiative should not be allowed to become so exaggerated as to imperil administration, the heart of the retail enterprise.

Policy should have the general objective of interlocking all interdependent subsystems. If there is no merchandising policy, advertising policy, and so on, there is little chance of achieving this objective.

It would be of value to also remember policy is not a declaration of concepts; it is a communication of a fact, a truth, a procedure everyone must adhere to. If orders for seasonal basic goods take six weeks to arrive in your store and the selling season lasts ten weeks, the coverage problem must be resolved into policy; it cannot be left to chance. If advertising is representing the whims of your merchandise manager, you, in truth, have no advertising policy to speak of. But if every department is considered important enough to receive its rightful share of advertising, you do have a policy. And when you have a policy, the most opinionated store manager or merchandise manager will adhere to it. If sales exceed budget and the operator or store manager decides to cut a large amount of budgeted ad expenditures, you again have no policy, but a critical variable instead. But if you advise all concerned that the programmed advertising percent (not dollars) is the mandatory figure to meet, you will have a policy that eliminates an action based on intuition. If the advertising percent is the mandatory requirement, then it would automatically be policy to increase the dollar ad expenditure when sales increase to bring the percent up to its budgeted figure. By the same principle when sales decrease by 10 percent, ad dollars must be cut by 10 percent to meet the budgeted ad ratio percent. This is policy.

Usage of policy, therefore, is a headquarters implicit strategem to insure that long-range advance promotional strategies will stay intact.

The two extremes,
too much stiffness in refusing,
and of too much easiness
in admitting any variation.
                    —The Book of Common Prayer

3

Creating the Implicit
Strategy Model

Once you have policy supporting your understanding of what
your business is, what it should be and what it can be, you can begin
to build your long-range implicit strategy structure. At this stage,
your base plan of strategy will not include the budgeting of advertising expenditures or the specific merchandising of items.

The only purpose is to assure our ability to perform at a future
time. When you develop the base plan, you are playing the role of
the president or chief executive of your enterprise—the entrepreneur, the master strategist. You want assurance that the prime selling times are noted and the key opportunities are internally communicated well in advance of the beginning of the selling period. In
addition to protecting prime selling times, strategy, at this early
stage, is necessary to attune everyone concerned, all of the subsystems, to the overall plan. Everyone must know where he is going,
when, and why.

As a retail strategist, our aim is cash flow and our target is near
money. Our first and true concern then is not isolated incidents—the

single advertisement—but instead in campaigns to move total inventory through the store before traditional selling times expire. Our new concern is "good-of-total-store," and because retailing is a *seasonal business enterprise,* our strategy campaigns will be better if molded to *seasonal* characteristics.

CONSTRUCTING THE STRATEGY PLANNING BASE

There are two natural promotional selling seasons in retailing. Each is planned and completed not less than six or eight weeks before the first promotional month of each season. Each season has its own characteristics. The first is the six-month period February through July; the second, August through January. Both begin with a month that opens a natural selling season and each ends with its own traditional clearance month.

Retail strategy then is a six-month proposition. Sales expectations (sales budgets) for each of the months within a season are noted and totaled (6 months = 100 percent). The percentage importance of each month's expected sales to the season total is charted as illustrated in Figure 4. Depending on the store type and size, sales budgets may be finalized by department or by lines of goods. This sales pattern chart, which will be used in later chapters, gives a clear-cut input and dramatizes our near money target times, the peaks and ebbs.

The underlying policy and control factors built into sales charting, the first step of our methodology, promote adherence to many of advertising's basic truths. The successful retail advertiser does not build a promotional thrust with item mistakes, overstocks, or soiled and damaged goods. Nor does he or she invest time or money in heavy promotion during normally slow times to create a non-traditional sales peak or simply improve sales during a slow period. The bulk of advertising dollars are placed where and when they will do the most good and the items offered in the advertisements are, to the best of the retailer's knowledge, all "winners". The idea is to improve performance during the traditional *good* selling times by inducing the consumer to shop in your store *first.*

Successful promotional methodology embraces the "winners" (items) and the "known" best selling times. But every retailer will make item mistakes (the items in inventory people have said they do not want), and every retailer will have overstocks and damaged goods. All of these must, of course, be cleared from inventory as

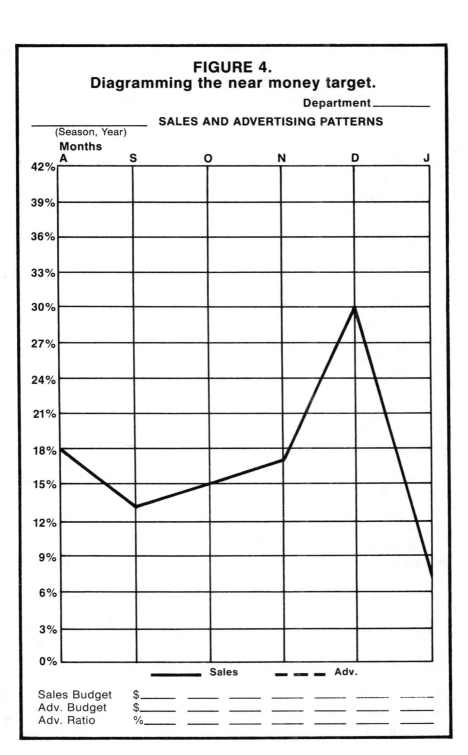

FIGURE 4.
Diagramming the near money target.

quickly as possible, but without influencing, cluttering, or weakening your "good-of-total-store" promotional strategy. There is a way to handle the problem.

First, exception is taken to one rule previously mentioned. There are some overstock items a retailer can, and very effectively, work into his ads. For example, a scrub bucket can be used as a traffic item (people producer) within a related time ad almost any time of the year. Nylons are another such item; both are year 'round basics. An overstock of either item can be corrected by constant attention and a temporary promotional price the consumer will pay. But a swimsuit on-hand overstock after the selling season ends is a different and more serious matter. If a store failed to run a closeout of swimsuits before the selling season came to an end, any advertising expenditure made to correct the inventory position would merely send good money after bad. With the required deep markdown, it would be a costly proposition. The same amount of dollar markdowns and monies spent to advertise wanted items will induce many more consumers to visit the store. A point to remember is that the strategist's prime attention is directed at the items specifically potent to the merchandise season he is in, and the strategist is acutely aware (item by item) that the season will soon pass.

An acceptable future for seasonal mistakes and old merchandise is one that follows a progressive markdown schedule. The idea is that there is a magic price a consumer will pay. The progressive markdown schedule budgets permanent progressive markdowns for a series of months or weeks. This procedure, *if adhered to* (many retailing people do not like to take markdowns), will control markdowns and also avoid a potential one-month markdown bath at a later time. The ticketed red-penciled items are pushed in the store by means of special display, special signing, and special personal selling efforts.

If the policy of progressive markdowns is followed, those items still on hand at the close of the six-month seasonal period will be near the magical price the consumer will pay, and, more important, these same items will make up the promotional power of traditional clearance ads (without the one-month markdown bath). It is true our initial promotional methodology pushes the loser items to the side, but it does so with a policy for their eventual liquidation. Do not be misled. Item mistakes are part of the business. If a retailer were correct 50 percent of the time, he would be stupendously successful, providing of course he knows how to get rid of the other 50 percent. Keeping inventories clean is a very important part of successful retailing, but it belongs largely to the first segment of managing, not to promotion.

At this point in constructing the strategy base, we have our sales budgets and the sales pattern of our departments or lines for a six-month period.

The next step is to finalize a six-month promotional calendar of events. There are several reasons for this step. First is control. We can anticipate the general pattern of business for our departments or lines of goods many months before a selling season begins. These particular times are important selling periods we cannot afford to miss. Whether a one-person enterprise or a 700-store chain, it would be prudent to zero in on the prime selling times that the sales pattern charts alert us to. The objective is to make these key periods the major part of our promotional program. Most retailers, for any month, will have one or two weeks' sales represent a significant large percentage of the month's total. During a major 10-day sale period (event) some stores may realize 70 percent of their total month's expected sales. It is strategically wise therefore to zero in on this 70 percent—the specific major selling time. The same is true of the importance of month to the total season. There are always one or two months in each season that will stand out.

These particular high sales months, in each of the two six-month seasons, are of chief concern to the strategist. Our first aim therefore, is to develop two major events, one for the spring and the other in fall.

The two very best events, historically, are grand openings and store closings. But these are one-time happenings. Next in sales potential is the anniversary sale, an event every store can and should schedule. The anniversary sale is the most legitimate excuse for a store to have a sale. If your store is less than five years old, a birthday sale banner is recommended, because it has a better credibility ring to it than "anniversary". The anniversary sale (or birthday sale) is of major importance; it is an event the retailer builds over the years. These sales are better scheduled in fall—September or October—or in spring—preferably April. However, much depends on your store and your market. The event must, of course, be scheduled for a season's traditional peak selling time, slightly before the peak, not precisely at the peak and, of course, not after it. Which-

FIGURE 5.
Common selling opportunities.

The Traditionals

February—July			August—January		
Feb.	Lincoln's Birthday	1*	**Aug.**	Back to School	31*
	St. Valentine's Day	4	**Sept.**	Labor Day	9
	Washington's Birthday	1		First Day of Autumn	9
Mar.	St. Patrick's Day	9	**Oct.**	Columbus Day	1
	First Day of Spring	9		Veteran's Day	1
Apr.	Easter (variable)	24		Halloween	9
	Mother's Day	9	**Nov.**	Election Day	9
May	Memorial Day	9		Thanksgiving	9
June	Armed Forces Day	1	**Dec.**	Chanukah	} 7 weeks
	Flag Day	1		Christmas	
	Father's Day	9		First Day of Winter	9
	First Day of Summer	9	**Jan.**	New Year's Day	4
July	Independence Day	9			

Clearance (January and July)—month long.

* Recommended duration (in days) of event. However, much depends on the day of the week that a particular holiday falls on in the calendar year.

ever season you select for the anniversary sale, it will become your major effort for that six months, excluding Christmas or Easter. Now you must determine another major effort for the six-month season that does not contain your anniversary sale. Here, too, you must schedule it for the prime selling time within the six months. For example, if yours is a hardware store, and you have scheduled your anniversary sale for October, you will want another major event for spring when the ducks are really flying, possibly in April. Spot it on the calendar (schedule it preferably for nine- or ten-day duration) and come up with a name for it. You will stick with this name year after year, and like the anniversary sale, you build it, you buy to it, year after year after year.

Now you have two major events of your very own, one for spring and one for fall. Two major selling opportunities have been anticipated and acknowledged.

The next step is to determine which of the remaining traditional retail selling opportunity times are for you. See Figure 5. Spot these times on the calendar and develop a name for them. There are times you should stick with the traditional. No store can beat the "George Washington's Birthday Sale" handle, or "Valentine's Day", "Memorial Day", "Independence Day", "Father's Day", or "Mother's Day" sales.

General merchandise stores could have a store-wide event each month, each scheduled for a four- or ten-day sale duration. The general merchandise store can do this, because in most every month it has lines or departments that peak. A store cannot, of course, create something that is not there.

The final step at this stage, after you determine the traditional themes you will go with, is deciding what types of events each will be.

TABLE 3-1.
Six basic event types.

EVENT	STRATEGY PURPOSE
1. Store-wide major	Seasonal peak selling effort
2. Store-wide	Advertising dominance
3. Departmental	Headquartership
4. Related departmental	Advertising dominance
5. Line	Good-better-best presentation
6. Related lines	Season and advertising dominance

There are different strategies for running each, and each will have specific time restrictions.

As implied earlier, a store-wide event is not scheduled when most departments or lines are not in or entering a peak selling time. And of course, store-wide events take considerably more time, personal effort, and dollar investment than a departmental event would. Store-wide events must be meaningful; if scheduled often and without just cause they will lose much of their credibility.

But the different event types, once recognized for what they are, will provide you ample opportunity to schedule a timely and interesting vehicle mix to suit your purpose. You will discover in later chapters how all strategic placements of event will center around or build up to the seasonal major store-wide effort.

Generally, the departmental event always represents a very important department in its peak selling period, with sufficient sales volume to support going it alone. Nine or ten days is the best dura-tion. However if the department has many seasonal lines peaking near the same time, a month-long campaign can be very meaningful. The extreme example is the toy department. The toy department campaign runs for three months. Its purpose, volume, and market leadership goal are established to match the season.

An example of a related department event would be paint and home modernization departments; furniture and floor covering; girl's, women's, and toddler's coats; or toys and Christmas trim. There are others. The only qualification is that they be naturally related departments that go well together. The purpose is to give newspaper lineage dominance with a united expenditure; when alone, each would be that much weaker. Nine or ten days is the best duration. Some, however, will be successful for a third week if the departments or items are seasonal big tickets, which usually require a longer buying decision time by the consumer.

The line promotion event is important to *maintain and expand* market penetration by a presentation of the good, better, best. Very often a store will fail to maintain this important image by consistent promotion of their low price point (good), or their top of the line (best); thus gradually reducing their true market potential. Depending on your line, of course, it is good to schedule a line pro-motion for each season. The promotion is developed as a campaign to run not less than ten days. The best duration is thirty days. It is important, again, to remember that at this stage of developing the basic promotional program for a season, we are not overly concerned with the nitty-gritty; all we want is assurance that our line of car batteries or what have you, which is extremely important to our spring (or fall) sales, will be given proper promotional attention when the specific selling time arrives. The specific tactics will be demonstrated in later chapters at the intrinsic strategy stage. An-other usage of the line promotion event, which will also be discussed later, is the development of a sleeper or sick department.

The omnibus promotion features store-wide traffic items. It is scheduled to the natural one-day sale opportunities generally dic-tated by holidays on a calendar. A one- or two-day duration is best; they do not work well for four, nine, or ten days. Omnibus promo-tions do not come up every month, but when they do they are too valuable a sales opportunity to pass over. Their purpose is to capture "plus" sales volume with store-wide traffic items—people producers.

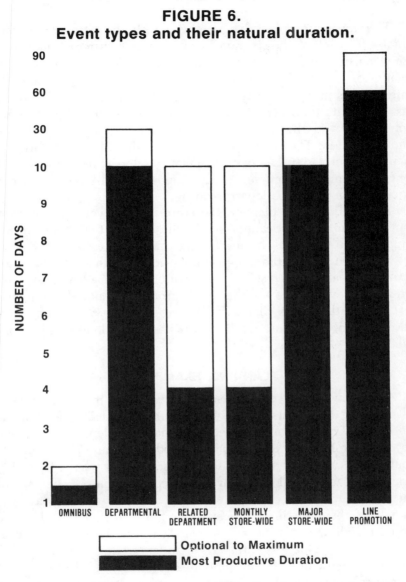

FIGURE 6.
Event types and their natural duration.

NUMBER OF DAYS

90
60
30
10
9
8
7
6
5
4
3
2
1

OMNIBUS   DEPARTMENTAL   RELATED DEPARTMENT   MONTHLY STORE-WIDE   MAJOR STORE-WIDE   LINE PROMOTION

☐ Optional to Maximum
■ Most Productive Duration

Events are vehicles to announce your anticipation of consumer needs and demands. An event mix is required, and depending on your store's personality, more or fewer will be scheduled. Sears, Penney's, and Wards are good examples of promotional stores; they would schedule considerably more events than a Fields or Neiman-Marcus. But the Fields and Marcus also have a mix; you have to look deeper to find it, because their approach is more genteel.

The strategist's objective is to establish the best promotional vehicles for each of the six months to announce anticipation of consumer needs. However, you cannot advertise your entire store. Because of the nature of the business, its many variables and the limited hours in a day, there is no retail store in the world that can mastermind its total needs and do everything right. There are not enough hours in the day nor are there ever enough experienced hands available. The headquarters planner should realize this fact. To pursue total day-in-day-out efficiency, department by department, is an unending pursuit of the impossible. The pursuit of perpetual motion would be less frustrating.

The headquarters planner, therefore, must develop the nucleus of a total campaign but cannot in all honesty expect 100 percent performance and efficiency from all departments. Therefore, the planner will zero in on the biggies for each month—the *important* departments and *major* selling opportunities. The idea is to make certain that everything for this small group of major departments, representing the larger share of the store's business, is given attention and help, and assurances that what is to be done will be done well.

PLANNING EXAMPLE

Assume we have received sufficient strategy input to proceed and pinpoint our events for the first month of a selling season, the month of February. The first step is to make a calendar worksheet. The calendar I prefer to use is illustrated in Figure 7. It helps to visualize the campaign strategy for the month as a whole. Carefully marking in the natural calendar holidays is a "must." The major influence of event placement are the days the natural holidays fall and where they fell in last year's calendar. Next, determine the number of selling days this year versus last year. Is there one additional Saturday? One less Saturday? One less or one more Monday? This knowledge will give you some idea of plus or minuses in reaching your sales budget. If a minus, you will have to make it up some way.

In the case of the general merchandise store, for example, my first suspicions would be that February would not lend itself very well to a major store-wide event; therefore, a supplemental event would be important. There are four opportunities, old traditionals,

FIGURE 7.
The strategist's calendar.

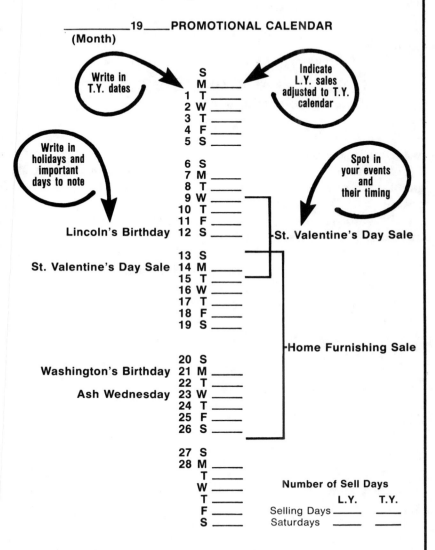

_____19____PROMOTIONAL CALENDAR
(Month)

Write in T.Y. dates

Indicate L.Y. sales adjusted to T.Y. calendar

Write in holidays and important days to note

Spot in your events and their timing

S
M
1 T ____
2 W ____
3 T ____
4 F ____
5 S ____

6 S
7 M ____
8 T ____
9 W ____
10 T ____
11 F ____
Lincoln's Birthday   12 S ____   St. Valentine's Day Sale

13 S
St. Valentine's Day Sale   14 M ____
15 T ____
16 W ____
17 T ____
18 F ____
19 S ____

Home Furnishing Sale

20 S
Washington's Birthday   21 M ____
22 T ____
Ash Wednesday   23 W ____
24 T ____
25 F ____
26 S ____

27 S
28 M ____
T ____
W ____
T ____   **Number of Sell Days**
F ____   **L.Y.   T.Y.**
S ____   Selling Days ____   ____
           Saturdays   ____   ____

The above planning calendar form can be easily duplicated. The only printed matter required is the actual calendar with the traditional holidays indicated. All other markings belong to the strategist. In later chapters, you will learn how this form is used in other ways to visualize advertising space and expenditures as total campaigns, for good-of-total-store.

and one or all lend themselves to promotion for most any kind of store:

1.　St. Valentine's Day sale (4 days, 2/9–2/12)
2.　St. Valentine's One Day Only sale (2/14)
3.　George Washington Day sale (4 days, 2/16–2/19)
4.　George Washington One Day Only sale (2/22)

Where would you place the major nine- or ten-day event? Or would you have one at all?

Consider these factors. Competition is keen in February. It's a tough month with no real seasonal reason for a total store-wide major.

I would pass consideration of a store-wide major for now, and see if anything else is of any importance. Review your event "type" list. Can any of these fit the traditional holidays?

There are several. One is the related department event.

Home furnishings departments, stereo, and TV are naturals for February. And searching for volume dollars, I would tie major appliances into it. All of the ad dollars for these departments combined could give sufficient lineage for a dominant campaign.

Where would you place it? Would you run it three weeks? Possibly February 2 through February 19? Or nine or ten days, February 2 through February 12?

Or is there a better slot? Consider all the factors you will be up against.

I would suggest a dominant campaign Wednesday (the best selling day in mid-week) through Monday.

I'll tell you my thoughts. The home furnishings and appliance event means important dollar volume, particularly in lean months. I must be certain I get my volume base, because it pays the salaries and the light bills. I'll need all the traffic help I can get for the good of other departments as well as big tickets. I want to get the most out of a small expenditure. The four supplementals, the traditionals, are all known traffic producers. With key items for each event, my store would be full. I'll shoot to hit near total store budgeted sales during that period. Four supplementals in one month is an unusual occurrence.

I would not have a major in February. Actually, all departments are participating, but they are under natural calendar banners. To have the store-wide major, I would have to drop the traditional sales banner or have it reduced to a subfeature line.

This is a good example of a "no no". Never, never fight naturals. Don't go on a creative kick trying to change a traditional; instead ride it for all it's worth.

Remember—we are acting in the capacity of the initial, implicit strategist at the top of the marketing plan. During this phase, we do not have to worry about filling up the holes. The important aim is our implicit strategy must be complete and firm.

Everything we have selected are naturals. The selling time is important for the particular department events selected. Once programmed, buyers will buy to it, stores will merchandise to it.

Our conclusion for February is four supplementals:

    1 related department
    3 departmentals

Why not go the entire month with the related department ad? Many do (not to imply they are wrong), but I wish to place additional sales goal emphasis (pressure) on the big ticket departments internally for the four *separate* events, not one major. This gives further insurance of success.

Having completed February, the same procedure is followed for the five remaining months of the six-month period. The natural calendar is considered first, then the important departmental or line peaks for that month.

March has one holiday, March 17. You may wish something to be done with it. A one-day supplemental? The omnibus ad?

April has Easter Sunday. This can cause some problem and push some Easter sales into March.

May has two holidays, Mother's Day and Memorial Day. June, Flag Day and Father's Day. July, Independence Day.

When or where to place your events depends on your business, your departmental selling patterns, and the sales characteristics of your particular market. My purpose is to demonstrate the mix our six event vehicles can contribute to a six-month calendar.

To best understand what we have accomplished with our advance calendar model, the question could be asked, "Can a store make a better one thirty days before the promotional month begins?" The obvious answer of course is negative! Remember, we are only talking vehicles and timing, not items and not competitive problems. We have acknowledged natural selling patterns and opportunities, we have only done what every store should do. We simply did not leave strategic timing to chance.

But more important, we now have an official six-month promotional vehicle that our planners can plan to, prepare internal communications for, create a required motivation force for, buyers can buy to, advertising and display departments can work and produce to, and a store can order promotional goods to with complete confidence.

By this simple programming, we have improved our competitive position and stabilized many critical variables.

4

Retailing's Natural Methodology

If we now know in advance what our timing (near money target) and what the promotional vehicles (events) will be, *we are ready then to consider the distinct competitive advantage of programming promotional goods to the event.* However, before any retailer can successfully adapt this policy, fundamental variables must be stabilized. And if we can gain greater insight into the economic value of time to the retailer, we can further appreciate the seriousness of our need for stabilization.

Primary stabilization is easily accomplished by pinpointing and publishing, or noting, for each of the promotional months within your six-month seasonal program, absolute deadline dates for each of the following items:

1. Promotional item candidate list

2. Promotional item release order date

3. Source ship date

4. Promotional item in-store date

Whether a small one-store operation or a chain of 700 stores, the functional requirements will be basically the same. You will either fulfill them all yourself or have many people do the various functions for you.

After you have finalized your six-month calendar of events (which does nothing more than firm up and list the sale start and end dates, the event name, purpose and the departments or lines of goods scheduled to participate), your next task is to develop a suggested promotional item candidate list for each month. The list is completed by month, some 90 or 120 days in advance of each promotional month. The time factor depends on your store type, size, sources of supply, ship factors, etc. The important point to remember is that there must be a six-month schedule of the candidate item list completion deadline date for each of the specific promotional months.

Why is a promotional item candidate list necessary? Why not simply merchandise each ad two or three weeks before its publication date, from existing inventory stock?

Remember our aim is managing. Ordering and merchandising are responsibilities every retail store has, but each function is different, and each requires time. Though all stores order goods, many do not function totally as a merchandiser. They do not use the full capabilities of this function, and this is the inefficiency, at the top of our model, that we are endeavoring to correct.

Preparation of the promotional candidate list is a buyer function. A meaningful list takes time whether the store is large or small. An actual search for item "winners" is required, special costs are tentatively negotiated, competitive shops are made, a host of other factors are considered before a list is decided on.

The strategist's objective is to engineer an item mix for good-of-total-store. This is merchandising. The buyer affords the merchandiser the opportunity to meet this challenge.

Figure 8 presents the autonomy of the promotional item program. The term "basics" in the illustration identifies those items regularly carried and reorderable in your store for a particular season or year. As a strategist, you will want to be certain, for each of your departments or lines, that the completed candidate list represents a proper mix of all four promotional item types.

The buyer's role therefore comes first, because no one can mer-

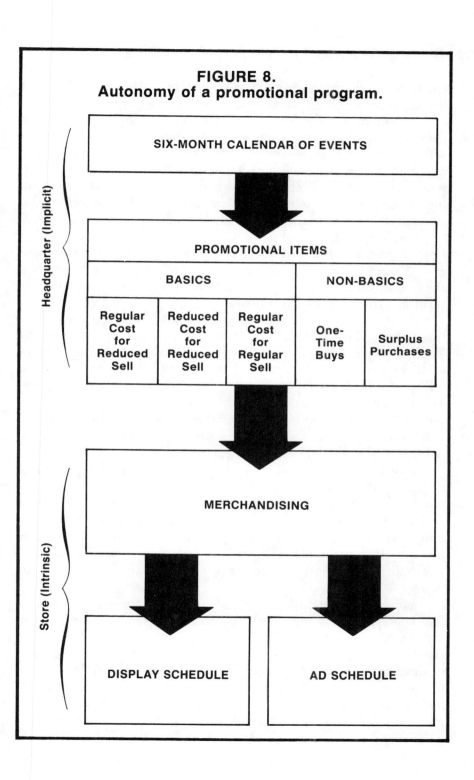

FIGURE 8.
Autonomy of a promotional program.

chandise intelligently, for good-of-total-store, until the merchandiser has a meaningful list of item candidates to select from.

A store promoting only non-basics (special purchases) will soon have an inventory and image of exactly that. A store offering best-selling basics at reduced selling with none secured at reduced costs may find the promotional markdowns an exceedingly heavy price to pay. And reduced selling of all items is not necessary. But there are highly seasonal, best-selling items already competitively priced that warrant only announcement to produce traffic in your store. A retailer, therefore, cannot profitably and effectively follow one type of item promotion. For a successful dominant program, there must be a mix. To get the mix, there must be control. And to have control, there must be time for review, and to be assured that you will have this time, there must be deadlines.

At this point, the model we are building represents a no-nonsense three-pronged attack of policy, decision-taking, and control. The consumer oriented marketing model and methodology we are discussing is a procedure of on-going managing systems and methods for the task of solving the retailer's constant concern—cash flow. The system rebukes excuses, promotes personal recognition, develops individuals, demands resourcefulness and self-reliance, coordinates and measures, in a common sense way, investment productivity against the retailer's actual cash flow.

This natural methodology is the management philosophy of the factual-positive—no fancies, no dreams, no miracles from advertising or individuals. Without retailing's natural methodology, there will be a diffusion of long- and short-range aims and a multiplying of individual self-objectives, a variety of unnecessary short-range risks, a nonexistent timetable, missed deadlines, missed sales opportunities, and never-ending changes of program, strategies, policies, and image.

For the promotional methodology to work, there must be absolute headquarters or top executive control. There are two major reasons for this requirement, other than stopping everyone from doing their own thing. The first and most important is the economic value of time to the retailer. The second reason is very broad, but is born of the first. Positive headquarters control assures confidence and makes possible the internal publication of a timetable. This in turn promotes the natural mechanics for blueprinting each monthly pro-

FIGURE 9.
Logistics of continuing requirements.

CONTINUING REQUIREMENTS

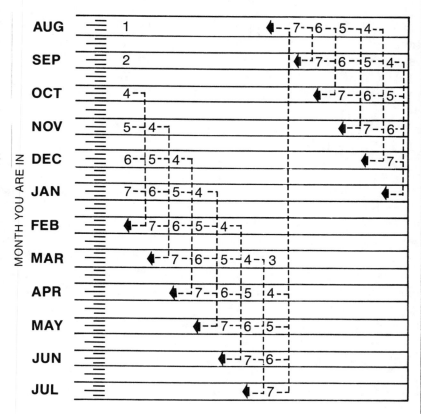

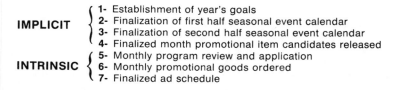

Key
◀ **Promotional Month Numerical Reference is made to**

IMPLICIT
{ 1- Establishment of year's goals
2- Finalization of first half seasonal event calendar
3- Finalization of second half seasonal event calendar
4- Finalized month promotional item candidates released

INTRINSIC
{ 5- Monthly program review and application
6- Monthly promotional goods ordered
7- Finalized ad schedule

With the exception of number keys 1-2-3, if you will read across in the month you are in, you will get some indication of the requirements you must meet for future promotional months.

motional vehicle many months in advance of the beginning of the promotional month.

To gain a deeper insight into the retailer's time problem, consider the basic requirements of each promotional month (Figure 9). Every retailer must face up to these requirements. The only variation will be in the amount of time required, which is related to a retailer's size (sales volume), and the shipping distance from sources of supply. Retailer "A" may require six to eight weeks to order and receive promotional goods before a promotional month begins; however, retailer "B" may only have to designate two days or two or four weeks. Regardless of the differences of time needs, time and deadlines for each promotional month are constant and known by every retailer. It will now become obvious that a meaningful and unchanging timetable must be developed to stabilize key planning dates, item candidate completion dates, and order due dates, just to mention a few. There are two elements you must know to complete your timetable and each can be easily determined from what we have already accomplished in Chapter 2. The first is the event time periods, the start and end dates of each. The second, determined from the first requirement is your shipping time. The shipping time is very important and should be accurate. If it takes three weeks to receive goods once the source has received your order, you will have to add time for preparing and mailing of orders, time for the review of item candidates, time for planning, and, if the promotional package comes from headquarters, additional time must be allowed to prepare the package. To establish the dates, work back from the start event date or the start of the specific promotional month. The first date to determine will be receipt of promotional goods into the store, just before the event begins.

To gain a still better understanding of the importance of retailing's constant deadline requirements, review Figure 10. Remember that the time factor will vary because of your type of store, your sources of supply, and your store size, but all of the requirements can be recognized as constant expectations, mandatory deadlines every retailer must meet. Figure 10 shows the same requirement needs as Figure 9, but identifies implicit and intrinsic strategy inputs.

There exists then a definite long-range planning requirement (implicit strategy) and the short-range firing line local merchandis-

FIGURE 10.
Strategy connections.

Promotional monthly implicit and intrinsic strategy input/output

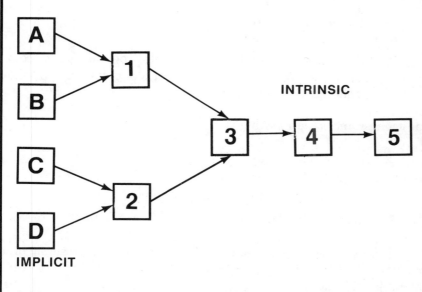

INTRINSIC

IMPLICIT

120 . . . . 100 . . . . 80 . . . . 60 30

DAYS BEFORE MONTH BEGINS

Key

IMPLICIT

A Six-month promotional calendar of events
B Marketing opportunities, promotional emphasis
C Promotional candidate items available to order
D Marketing norm expectations by department or lines

INTRINSIC

1 Finalization of promotional strategy and special emphasis
2 Ordering schedule and instructions regarding coverage policy
3 Department manager review and application
4 Promotional goods ordered
5 Ad schedule released to department managers

ing and advertising schedule requirement (intrinsic strategy). Obviously, there is a need for discipline.

Can any retailer bypass the determination of, or *deny* an authoritative date for completion of the following?

1. Season's sales budget
2. Seasonal event calendar
3. Headquarters month promotional program guide completed and released to all concerned before the promotional month begins.

For each promotional month:

4. Release order dates
5. Source ship dates
6. Promotional goods in-store dates
7. Month's ad schedule finalized

I have to believe most retailers already have some facsimile of a timetable. All that is being suggested is grouping and making a total timetable of deadlines mandatory as seasonal policy before the season begins.

Once you have completed a timetable of your mandatory dates for a six-month period and have reviewed it, you will quickly discover there are probably many other dates you will have to add. If you must have the first half seasonal program done by a certain date, you will have to schedule an initial planning meeting date and a follow-up review date. Keeping in mind the retailer's dollar investment in inventory and the purpose of our strategy and advertising, our timetable can be better appreciated as a stabilizer, and also as a means of preventing procrastination.

From a purely financial point of view, it would make sense to take precautions that the promotional goods arrive in the store neither too early nor too late. Both errors will affect your inventory turnover and your open-to-buy, and if the problem grows, your strategy program will have to be junked. Can we agree then, regardless of how small your business may be, on the need for deadlines?

At this point, you should begin to see how the methodology parts begin to interlock. Most important is how the implicit strategies and control are natural initiative requirements at the top of the marketing plan.

Figure 11 diagrams the basic communication flow of the total promotional plan. At the top is the strategist, representing top executive management (SM). The tactics are established for each six-month period as they are developed in their order, spring (ST) and fall (FT). This six-month plan for each is developed by working with top management buying, merchandising, display, and advertising people. Before proceeding further, it is important to remember what the six-month plan is and what it is not. The six-month plan establishes events, the timing of events, and their strategic importance to the achievement of headquarters goals. The events finalized are mandatory, locked in, and not subject to change. The plan is not, at this particular stage, a merchandising or item commitment. Very simply, it presents the events that will run and establishes the headquarters long-range *strategy* and *deadline* timetable. When a six-month plan is completed, it is distributed to the planners of the organization. It is also distributed to store managers so they can complete their own six-month event program for spring strategy (SS) and fall strategy (FS). At headquarters, from the six-month plan, the buyers, advertising people, merchandisers, display, all work toward the development of the monthly event package. These monthly packages are numbered 1 through 12 on the chart.

The store tailors the monthly plan to its local market and orders the items they have elected to advertise. We now have implicit strategy and intrinsic, centralization with decentralization.

We have progressed very quickly over a multitude of important, complex retailing approaches and functions. We have elected to separate the promotional activities from the general business of retailing; we have instituted the need for and idea of a timetable and have followed the procedure for the establishment of six-month promotional plans. Our progress so far has stabilized many critical variables, but these cannot become real until the most important policy of all is established.

If we consider Figure 3 again, then Figure 9, we will gain fresh insight into the scope of the next problem to be resolved. Who controls it all? Who or what department is the central control center for the promotional side of the business? Who is the central communicator?

Before we discuss this problem, the reader should be warned

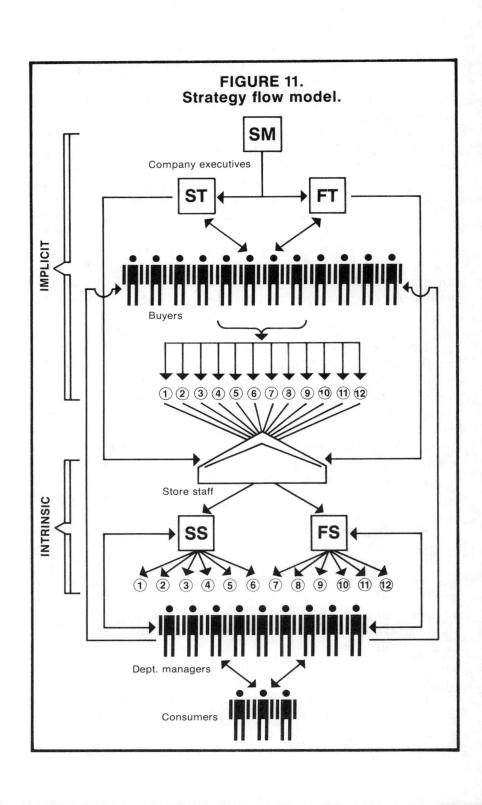

**FIGURE 11.
Strategy flow model.**

not to compare the upcoming recommendations with the present performance and limitations of the organization you now have. You may feel we are talking about some reorganization that would be impossible with your present staff capabilities or numbers. We are not talking about the reorganization of people. The inefficiencies of many individuals or departments are not generally personal but are caused by the system that exists, or the nonexistence of a system. If walls are built around the merchandising or the advertising departments, the people in each will never be able to function totally. A proper change of systems and methods, in my experience, can change a department to one of great efficiency. Managing, which is policy, decision-taking, and control, works on the principle of no individual is indispensable. This is not derogatory to the individual because individuals can think, machines or systems do not. But to secure the greatest contribution from individuals or yourself, there must be order. In other words, the very worst advertising department in the world may quickly prove to be the most efficient, with the correct systems and methods.

The natural selection for a central communicator/controller is the advertising department. Examine Figure 2 again to see a picture of advertising's mainstream influence. There are additional reasons for this recommended selection. First, advertising is the only department in the retail structure, other than the president, that never has reason *not to* have the "good-of-total-store" at heart 100 percent of the time. In addition, all of the pieces that make up an effective advertising and promotion program must come from all departments within the retail structure *to* the advertising department. Each of these pieces represents "needs" of the advertising department. If a retailer has permitted walls to be built around its merchandise departments to protect them from advertising harassment, then advertising's function of overall coordination will be nonexistent.

The advertising department, as an extension of the president, therefore must be able to communicate its needs, police what is given, and enforce adherence to the president's policy and deadlines. The first policy to enforce and deadline to establish will be the completion of a six-month planning schedule. It begins with a plan to plan.

When policy is decided, the advertising department or a specific individual can act as a control center and promotional communicator and coordinator, thus laying the groundwork for stabilizing personal

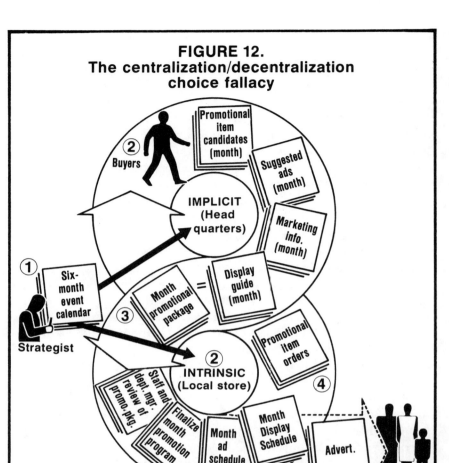

FIGURE 12.
The centralization/decentralization choice fallacy

The question above is not for a retailer because there is no such thing as decentralization or centralization in successful retailing. There is, of course, if you relate what your arm is to your body and relate what centralized buying is to the total enterprise. If you cut off your arm, it would indeed be decentralized, as would the buying function if it were cut off to a simple singular function of buying. In both instances, the body would not be able to function at its full potential. The difference between the top managing task and the bottom is in strategy. It's as easy to achieve as counting 1 to 5, if you know the secret. The key is in the six-month calendar of events. When this is meaningful, complete, mandatory and everyone in the organization knows the calendar will not change, each promotional month can be intelligently developed, and each of the subsystems programmed to it. The secret is to count 2 twice. At the time you release the six-month calendar to your headquarter planners also release a copy to each of your store managers. You see the general policy and control is at the top management level. The decision-taking is at the bottom. This is managing.

independent buyer promotional activities. The seriousness of this variable is measured by the size of the retail establishment or company. For a small, very small store, the manager simply talks to himself, but even this personal conversation should be disciplined. One will begin to relate not to the individual problems, but strategy for "good-of-total-store." This will be the "overview" of the strategist. The strategist will begin to see correct answers and there will be better decision-taking. For the larger company, a chain for example, it would mean a branch store will not receive independent promotional ideas and communications from some thirty or forty different merchandise or buying departments (some being received a week in advance of a promotional month, others two days after the month, but never the same schedule from month to month). For any store manager to finalize a dominant strategy from thirty or forty different strategists would indeed be a miracle.

It is evident then, that there must be time for review and coordination; there must be time for a store to order and receive goods. If a retailer fails to meet functional time requirements, can he truly expect efficiency and an effective advertising program? I think not. I have personally witnessed large companies (one with 100 million and another with billions in sales), and smaller companies, that send their promotional program to a store without allowing time for the store to order the promotional goods scheduled for the event. I have seen advertising materials completed or arrive the night before or the day before an ad is scheduled to run. That the president of any company can allow any individual to fail in fulfilling these very basic but extremely important retailing requirements is a mystery of our times. Stranger still, is that the store manager and department manager are the individuals usually criticized for the store's poor performance. But, this is the reason we are suggesting policy; decision-taking is not generally late or missed because of its own discretion (there are exceptions), but instead the lateness is caused by unstabilized critical variables at the top of the marketing model —namely the buying, merchandising and/or central advertising function. And to top management who are told lateness of advertising is the nature of the business, our message is—don't believe it. There are, and always will be important item and other changes for one reason or another that happen at the very final phase of the advertising function. But these represent a small percentage, some

20 percent, of change when the program adheres to its implicit strategy, policies, and deadlines.

There are certain promotional policies to be developed to protect your merchandising and advertising aims. Only you can determine what image your store should have. But whatever you desire it to be, this information must be spelled out in writing. There must be a bulletin issued for each specific policy developed. The important point made in a previous chapter is that policy must be adhered to. A manager of a store cannot order a department manager or the advertising manager to advertise "seconds" when this is against company policy. Nor can the store manager dictate false advertising claims to the advertising manager if this is against company policy. And the manager cannot elect not to run a major company event, nor can a buyer refuse to participate, if company policy requires mandatory adherence.

Whatever your company policy may be, it must be spelled out. Verbal policies are detrimental to your success, and are seldom, if ever, adhered to. If promotional policy is not understood, the methodology will not work, because both the strategy and the advertising vehicle have to come and be supported from top to bottom. If promotional policy is not adhered to at the bottom of the marketing model, then earlier commitments become meaningless and additional risks are created, because you end up with two or more plans, not one. My own experience has told me that managing failure does not occur at the bottom of a company structure; it has always proved itself to be at the top.

With retailing's natural methodology, a buyer cannot command a store to have an event for the buyer's particular department. The buyer can suggest the departmental or item promotion to the headquarters strategist or planner, but if the recommended event is not placed on the company's six-month calendar, it is not to run. There can never be separate promotional communications to the store about promotions that are not on the calendar. A company promotional calendar can be sufficient vehicle for any store to advertise their wares. All the company is doing is naming the event and scheduling it for a promotional period of time that is most probably the same time any local store would schedule it. The methodology also prohibits some forty departments from going their own separate ways. All must go under the store-wide event banner and support it. There are, of course, exceptions for departments that peak during a particular month; they will have individual headquarters scheduled events, but generally, all participate in the major event. If there is no comprehensive six-month calendar, however great your headquarters implicit strategy may be, critical variables will always persist and an uncoordinated activity remain.

We have implied that the local store, for a particular promotional month, must have the right to reject or accept promotional item candidates suggested by the buyer. And, the manager should also have the freedom to order the desired item in any quantity. This is decentralized decision-taking, but the takings (goods ordered) must be known to the headquarters company buyer.

Yet, while the local store manager can elect or reject promotional items and quantities, he or she must have good reason for whatever action taken. There must be a feedback of the manager's decisions to the headquarters buyer. Many times the local manager will substitute the buyer's recommendation with another item. And the buyer will have to order quantities of the manager's substitution to support the advertisement. All business being local, the manager's decision may very well be correct, but should be evaluated by headquarters.

We now have some hint of the ingredients of the methodology, and why success will vary by degrees, company to company.

Systems and methods do not create strategy, profit, turnover, or cash flow—people do. Methodology only increases the possibility of success by stabilizing critical variables. This, in turn, allows employees to carry out the implicit strategy of the headquarters strategist.

DANGER POINTS

It is important to consider other non-promotional retailing areas that will seriously influence your strategy and control program. A store must, of course, be in stock on all of its basics, certainly never less than 90 percent. There has to be a counting schedule and rhythm in ordering to assure this condition. And though we are speaking mainly of promotional goods in this book, there are also seasonal coverages and these too must represent a good in-stock condition. A store then has three coverage policies to resolve: seasonal, promotional, and day-to-day replenishment of the basics. When any one of the three is consistently below 90 percent in stock, the greatest strategy program in the world will do little for you. Your death may be slow, but it will be certain, because, regardless of how much importance may be placed on strategy or promotion, your inventory is the cause of your success. It is the "good thing", your reason for being. "Lows" and "out of stocks" cause you trouble. The problem is usually due to a lack of a coverage policy, a responsibility within the first managing segment of your business.

We have come far, and we have gained some insight into the dangers of the basic business of retailing. And if you are beginning to suspect that it isn't the easiest business in the world, chances are good you will make retailing's natural methodology and systems work to make strategy a reality for your store.

We do not what we ought;
What we ought not, we do;
And lean upon the thought
That chance will bring us through;
But our own acts, for good or ill,
Are mightier powers.
                                    —Matthew Arnold

5

CONTROL:

Stabilizing the Variables

When is a system "in control"?

There are several identifying marks. One is a steady output. Another is smoothness. Smoothness, however, has many implications. For the retailer daily activity is indeed hectic, and it always will be. But when there is stability of long-range implicit headquarters strategies, when the strategies are maintained without need of special measures or panic to achieve results, when there is no major change of program or policy—then you have smoothness of system.

We have already discussed many means of gaining some stability and some smoothness of system. But these means do not govern —they give some, but not complete, control. We said we should program our events by season, in advance of the season. But how many events? And how much in promotional markdowns should be allocated? How can one know that all departments are doing their job to the best of their ability, for good-of-total-store?

To accomplish this task, there must be continuous and automatic comparisons of system behavior against a standard and continuous and automatic feedback of corrective action. This is not new. The problem facing many managers is how to do it.

The trick is to manage your business by a comparison to norms. The *exceptions* to these norms get management attention.

If a retailer could establish, for his or her own knowledge, norms for certain components, and then create reports as quickly as possible at the close of each promotional month giving the actual figures achieved, automatic feedback of performance to the norm would be achieved. He or she would be able to immediately give attention to the exceptions.

You will need three monthly reports. One is a report card for merchandise performance, another for advertising and, of course, a daily sales report. Listed below are the basic components of each report. You may wish to add some or reduce the number.

Departmental (or Line) Merchandise Comparison Report

Department or line identification
Actual net sales: this year—last year
% of increase/decrease
Sales budget: month—next 3 months
Closing inventory: actual—budget
On order
Markup % on inventory
Sales returns ($'s)
Markdowns ($'s): promotional—permanent
Markups ($'s)
Discounts and allowances
Old merchandise ($'s)—year to date

Departmental (or Line) Advertising Report

Department or line identification
Actual net sales: this year—last year
Advertising expenditure ($'s): this year
Advertising % to sales
Year to date sales: % of increase/decrease
Year to date advertising % to sales
(On the back of the report, give a breakdown of total advertising expenditure by media and other non-media areas, i.e., advertising payroll, art, printing, etc.)

Daily Sales Report by Department (or Line)

Department or line identification
Daily net sales: this year—last year
Month to date net sales: this year—last year

The contents of your reports and the different kinds you may need will, of course, depend on your size and your type of retail store. You do not wish to overburden yourself with reports, but every store will require something similar to these three tools to effect control. The norms can be found in trade journals or through your trade organization. There are many other figures a sophisticated retailer will use, but our model covers only the major points necessary to get the system to function.

Most retailers are well aware of the importance of sales budgets, but to those of you who have very small stores or are new to the industry, a few words on the subject may be of some benefit.

Sales budgets are necessary for control of your expenditures. They represent the "must" actual net sales figure you seek to attain each month. All expenditures are based on and restricted to the sales budget because much of what a retailer spends is in advance of an actual sale. It would be impossible to plan without a sales budget and it would also be impossible to control and measure your performance. The sales budget is arrived at by considering many factors, and it is generally a conservative figure, representing an inflation-adjusted increase over the sales of the previous year. The general range of increase will vary by store and circumstances. And, of course, there are occasions a decrease is budgeted. Trends, an increase or decrease, alert you to the direction you will take. A six- or eight-week trend of a 10 percent sales decrease in a line of goods would not encourage a budgeted increase in sales for any upcoming month. There are many, many reasons for sales increases and sales decreases. To cover them all would require another book. The point is that the sales budget is a "must" to effect control of the variables and, of course, an initial necessity for construction of your strategy plan.

In addition to sales budgets there must also be a plan to plan. There must be a planning schedule with specific meeting dates; each must be communicated to all concerned. These dates are carefully arrived at and checked out with each person required to attend the meetings to be certain that the particular date is cleared on his or her calendar. Once the schedule dates are published, they cannot be changed and all scheduled for attendance must attend.

This is important because, as we have mentioned in previous chapters, time has immense economic value to the retailer. Much has to be done before the actual promotional month is upon you. If there is procrastination, you can bet it will cost you in lost sales and, of course, do little to stabilize the variables.

Your advance planning schedule would look something like this. The aim is to complete a six-month promotional calendar of events which can be accomplished in one meeting or six. The bottom half of the schedule deals with merchandising and item candidates on an individual month-to-month planning basis.

TABLE 5-1.
Sample of advance planning schedule.

SIX-MONTH PLANNING SCHEDULE, SPRING

Promotional Month:	FEB	MAR	APR	MAY	JUN	JUL
Planning guidance and letter released to participants	___	___	___	___	___	___
Planning meeting	___	___	___	___	___	___
Review meeting	___	___	___	___	___	___
Final review	___	___	___	___	___	___
Six-Month Calendar Released						___
Monthly guides and promotional item candidates released to store	___	___	___	___	___	___
Promotional item release order date	___	___	___	___	___	___
Source ship date	___	___	___	___	___	___
Promotional item in-store date	___	___	___	___	___	___

A six-month event calendar must be completed before you can plan the merchandising for the first promotional month of that season. Why not just do it month to month? The reason is that then every month would become an original new planning meeting for promotional events as well as merchandising. If we recognize retailing as a seasonal business, it would be to your advantage to give each of your staff and store managers a road map for the season. The six-month calendar is that map. It eliminates changes or new starts, and affords you the opportunity to establish some kind of order by the use of deadlines. Some readers may feel this six-month event information would leak out and place the store in a vulnerable position. The information will, of course, leak out—to a very small degree—but you must understand it is only a calendar of events with the timing indicated, the name of the event, and the departments which will participate in each. It does not have any information about prices or items or media. It only tells what every retailer already knows. You will have an event for Valentine's Day, for George Washington's Birthday, and so on. The traditional holiday times are the best times to promote, and everyone does. The strength of the six-month calendar is that it stabilizes variables. But it will not happen if you do not have a mandatory, absolute unchangeable planning schedule.

Headquarters will often times miss the sixth item on your planning schedule. The reason for this procrastination is that headquarters people, not unlike people working in the stores, have many things to get done. There are certain things they must do and get done for their own health, so other things are pushed off. If your organization is made up of some forty departments, it would indeed be a task to have all materials in on time to meet one deadline mailing date. Many cannot accomplish the task. There is only one cure I know of. If top management allows you to use it, just once, mail the package on the scheduled date, *regardless of how many departments are missing*. If any did miss your deadline, you can be assured they will not miss again. When the decision is made to go with what you have, it usually leaks out to the staff and there is suddenly a flood of materials on the coordinator's desk. The importance of this date may not be recognized by others in the company, outside of the president and the strategist. But all one has to do to consider its value is recall the variables it stabilizes.

Another variable problem is receipt of promotional goods in the store. Considerable time can be wasted if these goods are not properly identified to the event and stored for that particular time. Failure to do so is a serious threat to your strategy and advertising credibility. This problem can be somewhat resolved by having a place on your purchase order for an event code. This will alert your receiving

FIGURE 13.
Implicit strategy doctrine.
WHY IMPLICIT CONTROL?

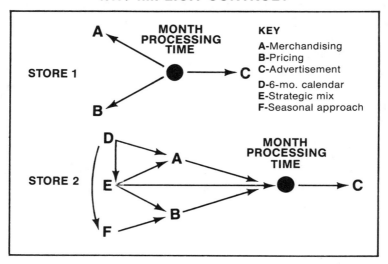

KEY

A-Merchandising
B-Pricing
C-Advertisement

D-6-mo. calendar
E-Strategic mix
F-Seasonal approach

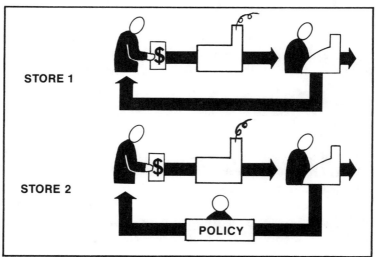

If you want to visualize how much your advance planning methodology actually accomplished, review the top section of this figure. Which of the two stores will have the competitive edge?

And in the lower section, which of the two will have more certainty of smoothness vs. wild fluctuations?

room that the goods are to be keyed to or stored in some particular area. It also will help when the department manager reviews the open order file; the event will be identified and earlier action can be taken to prevent a late shipment. Many retailers, of course, already have quite adequate systems to solve the problem. But it is important that the new retailer remember to receive promotional goods before the event and place them in a hold area.

At this stage of our development, it would be worthwhile to consider what has been eliminated.

We have eliminated headquarters independent departmental promotional guidance, letters, conversations, etc., generally made every day and any day throughout a month. We have eliminated the need for the headquarters chief executive to ask a store manager, "What do you have going for this month?" Instead, during a store visit, the executive will ask, "What have you done about the 'Paint Jamboree' that starts next week? Let me see your plans." The president can ask the same question of the buyer from the headquarters office one month or six months before the event begins. Most important, your monthly package to stores will be more informative, giving the store manager and department manager knowledge they can use to their advantage.

There are other variables to be stabilized, to be sure, and previous chapters have presented ideas for stabilizing many of them. The following chapters will show means of stabilizing others, and there are many more you are well aware of, variables not mentioned. But with a yardstick of norms and a six-month calendar, control and smoothness will be easily within your reach.

*The business of
America
is business.*

—Calvin Coolidge

6

Strategic Expansions
and Contractions

There is another important part of our model to consider before
strategy can become fully productive. Floor space, like newspaper
space, is merchandised to effect sales volume, turns, and profits. Sell-
ing-floor space comes under the general business of retailing, the first
segment, but there is a part of it, because of particular seasonal characteristics, that greatly influences the promotional side of our activities. I am talking about the highly seasonal departments requiring
major expansions on the selling floor during specific long selling periods.

During their seasonal selling peaks, these select departments or
lines of goods will be the heart and driving force of your promotional strategy. This is known, and can be anticipated a year or longer
in advance. Because of their strategic importance to the total promotional program, the programming of the major seasonal departments is a "must" task. Seasonal departments are promotional giants
because their selling periods are defined—there is a specific, gradual
beginning on the calendar and an abrupt, clear-out sudden ending.

For example, consider the "toyland" department. It is traditional for a retailer to have his complete toy department set up by

the middle or end of October. The abrupt end of the toy selling period is the week before Christmas. The Christmas trim shop is generally scheduled for complete set up in the early part of November, and its abrupt end is three or two weeks before Christmas. Lawn and garden has a beginning and an end. Candy, lingerie, and men's furnishings are other departments that call for major expansions.

Because the beginning and end of a seasonal selling period can be pinpointed, the determination of goods, broader assortments, and additional above-normal quantity needs for this specific period can be approached as you would approach an event. You must get in and get out quickly. To realize this aim, at the time you make your item determinations, you should also write your advertising schedule. This affects the strategy for the total store. The major departmental seasonals cannot be left to chance.

My experience has taught me that proper programming and setting up of seasonal departments is not easy. One way to do it is to make the major departmental seasonals a specific and official part of the headquarters implicit promotional strategy program, listing them on your six-month promotional calendar with a start and end date. By doing so, personal involvement will begin early; a program will evolve. Expectations and commitments will be resolved, resulting in a greater possibility of proper headquarters follow-through and feedback. With the total involvement as part of the promotional program, a separate guide or checklist for stores can be developed which will tie merchandising and advertising together.

Some of the tips included in a typical guide would be the following:

1. Merchandise Marketing Guide

    a. *Normal* line sales percent to total department expectation

    b. Special items recommended to broaden lines

    c. Special promotional item recommendations

    d. List of probable best sellers

    e. High gross profit items highlighted

    f. Recommended percent of total sales for promotional goods

    g. Industry trends and reasonable sales expectations

h. Consumer activity

i. Competition input

j. Liquidation of slow mover item start-date and suggested markdown schedule

k. Worksheet completion date and mailing to headquarters

2. Department Floor Expansion Plans and Models

a. Small, medium, large floor plans (S-M-L)

b. Inventory investment (S-M-L)

c. Display model sketch or photos of line presentations

d. Display fixture guide

e. Coverage worksheet, item by item, line by line

3. Ordering Schedule

a. Initial order release date

b. First reorder release date

c. Second reorder release date

d. Cut-off date

4. Department Display Set-Up Schedule

a. Start date

b. Completion date

c. Down date

5. Advertising Program

Some examples of the major seasonal department types we are talking about are the following:

Department	Expansion	Contractions
Sporting goods	Spring	June
Toys	October	December 20
Christmas trim	November	December 15

Slippers for the family	November	December 21
Men's furnishings	November	December 26
Candy	October	December 26
Lingerie	October	December 26
Women's accessories	October	December 26

There are others; only the retailer's sales expectations can tell which will require more space to correspond to its heavier promotional effort and which will require less. If a department does 70 percent of its year's business in November and December, it is obvious that at this time it will spend more ad dollars and require additional space. An exception would be the department that already has sufficient space which was considerably wasted the other ten months of the year; this situation would require no expansion—only a better job.

THE MAGIC SEVEN WEEKS BEFORE CHRISTMAS

No selling season compares to Christmas. It is best to have your merchandise ready, item by item, by the second week in November. Christmas decorations should be up, complete, by three days before Thanksgiving. By placing emphasis on your Christmas items the second week of November, you will have some clues as to your very best sellers. You may possibly have time to reorder these items and have them in your store the first week of December. But more important, with the early deadline, you are assured of being ready the day before Thanksgiving.

Many stores do not have the opportunity to expand key Christmas lines. But they may be able to squeeze in an extra fixture or two. These will produce "plus" volume. Or you may only be able to give special emphasis to key fixtures and space you already have. The point to remember is Christmas arrives very quickly and leaves very quickly. The opportunities afforded you in this short time are only restricted by the merchandising restocking time you give your counters. One idea successfully used to make the most of your selling time and opportunities is what I call the "feature end" program or "single item tonnage features". It accomplishes two things, both resulting in "plus" sales. First, it will make your store interesting with little effort. Second, it will promote key items that you can sell in depth.

FIGURE 14.
Fixture strategy

FEATURE FIXTURE SCHEDULING
Rough sketch of floor plan first, number key fixtures.

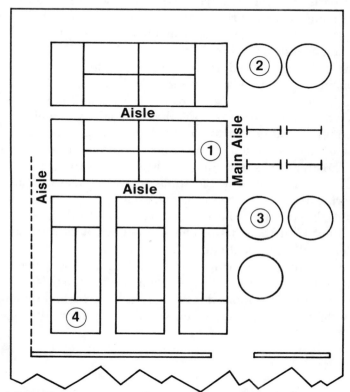

Merchandise your key fixtures by item, by date.

EVENT	FIX. END NO.	ITEM	SELL		UP DATE	DOWN DATE	Start Count	End Count	Comment
			Reg.	Sale					

The idea is to designate key locations or end fixtures you can change once a week. The trick is to draw a rough sketch of your fixture arrangement and number the special fixture or end fixtures you will designate as features. Then merchandise them on a week-to-week basis on a form similar to the one shown in Figure 14. You cannot change your entire department or store once the Christmas selling season begins, but you can change one fixture, or two or three, each Monday.

The point presented in this brief chapter is that expansion departments represent a unique and golden selling opportunity. The less you leave to chance, the more you merchandise, and the better you keep on top of your inventory, the more sales you will reap.

Too often a store fails to reduce the selling area of a non-Christmas department to expand its neighbor. Girdles and bras are certainly not Christmas lines, but lingerie, dusters, and robes are. Building materials are not the best Christmas gifts, but many items in the neighboring hardware department are. Shoes are not a Christmas item, but slippers are. File folders, paper, and other office supply lines are not Christmas items, but typewriters, desk sets, and many other items within the stationery department are.

Your expansion departments are the natural heavyweights for the season; they therefore represent your promotional "sock". When your advertising is supported with a logical corresponding emphasis on the selling floor, your effectiveness will be dramatically increased.

If you would hit the mark,
you must
aim a little above it.
—Henry Wadsworth Longfellow

7
SALES GOALS:
The Perpetual
Front Line Objectives

Strategic expansions and contractions are extremely important to your overall strategy effectiveness; with them, your implicit long-range program is nearly complete. There is one more magical ingredient to add at the headquarters implicit strategy level. The task is truly a local store activity, but it is of such great importance to total company performance, that it, too, cannot be left to chance.

There are two popular labels used to identify a retailer's monthly sales expectations. One previously mentioned is the sales budget; the other is the sales goal. The two, in retailing circles, have different meanings. The monthly sales budget is the official anticipated sales for a department or line of goods. It's a "must" figure, usually conservative, and generally based on a slight increase over last year's actual sales for the same period. Current economic trends greatly influence the sales budget decision. In turn, all operating and advertising budgets are developed and restricted to the sales budget.

The sales goal is not a budget figure; it is a personal commitment to management for sales in *excess* of the sales budget. The commitment is made by the individual in the store responsible for a line of goods or a department. The *expenditure* necessary to achieve this commitment, however, is not *to exceed the dollar amount dictated by the sales budget.* The trick is that any sales budget can be exceeded by 5, 10, or 15 percent, depending on the department, without requiring new and higher inventory budgets.

The sales goal is the hidden force behind all successful retailing strategies, and makes the difference between one general merchandise store realizing $54 per square foot of selling space and another "similar" store racking up $100 or $200 per square foot.

But . . .

The magical power in capturing consumer dollars in excess of sales budgets and greater sales per square foot of selling space is not the personal commitment made by the department manager, though the commitment's importance is very great. The trick is prodding your department manager to dig. And when one digs, magic begins to happen; you begin to merchandise to consumer needs. Because, as when he or she prepares sales budgets, the experienced department manager/retailer will first look to where the "plus" sales can be achieved before any goal commitment is made.

Our department manager knows how to scratch for the clues that lead to improvement and untapped sales opportunities. That's what daily retailing growth is all about—improvement. The department manager is the master sleuth in capturing increases. Only the manager can organize the lab to decipher the *facts* from intuition. And this is begun by holding all lines suspect for above-normal increases.

A request for sales goals commitments then, for the headquarters purpose, provides some assurances that merchandise people will dig and in so doing, will merchandise their key lines or departments in advance, one new month after another, to anticipate the demands and needs of the consumer.

But the simple request for a sales goal commitment is not adequate by itself. Top management has got to give the clues.

A request for a sales goal commitment is not always sufficient to move or inspire your people, and to leave the outcome to chance would be detrimental to your general well-being. If however, some clues are given to where "plus" sales may be found, favorable response can be more realistically expected. In addition to the clues some form of program or yardstick should be given to inspire meaningful comparison to norms.

What are the clues to "plus" sales opportunities? Where can the opportunities be found? It is difficult to say exactly for every particular store, because the times and local opportunities will vary line by line, item by item, and department by department. But there are always the traditional basics that will supply an adequate number of clues for any department manager to discover "plus" sales sources.

The discovery of:

1. *Sleeper items and/or lines of goods*
   Items or lines that have sold very well with little or no attention.
2. *Missed seasonal opportunities*
   The traditional, previously overlooked.
3. *Promotional markdown inactivity or deficiency*
4. *Abnormal selling pattern*
5. *Below norm departments or lines*
6. *Ranking deficiencies*

Each of the six categories will lead you to discover "plus" sales opportunities. You will, however, need yardsticks or norms to make meaningful comparisons. Securing the necessary figures would be no problem for a chain, but the one-store operator, mentioned in previous chapters, will have to look to his trade associations and the specific trade publications. Either of these can provide the adequate norm figures to place your own against. This comparison indicates the areas for improvement. The result of any improvement is "plus" sales; sales you would not have gotten otherwise.

For example, if, in a typical store in the housewares industry, sale-priced items equal 20 percent of total monthly sales, but your department's "sale item" percentage of sales is 7 percent, it would be evident some additional sale items (*wanted items*) and promotional markdowns will produce additional traffic and volume. If, in your store, your men's furnishings department's spring season sales peak in May and the industry peaks in June, you more likely than not have "plus" sales opportunities in June. If your hardware department ranks number 12 in volume in your store but in the industry, for "like" stores, the department ranks number 6, you can rightfully suspect "plus" sales opportunities exist for your department. The traditional and seasonal opportunities that exist year after year also provide opportunity.

In your research you may discover a department with a multitude of serious deficiencies, all adding up to failure to secure your rightful share of market.

Such discoveries may add up to a realistic expectation of 30–50 percent increase. Here is a golden opportunity for "plus" sales, but it is, however, one that calls for new budgets, a new rebuilding of the department's merchandise, and again, not necessarily more space. To get the sick department where it should be, in relation to the industry, you must work out a three- or six-month priority campaign for the department. The campaign, to be successful, cannot merely vocalize your personal ideas or independent (non-related) promotional efforts, but instead must present the merchandise story of the department; a story, evidently, not previously told. We will discuss its importance to the strategy role in the following chapters.

The below-norm department will need:

1. A higher than average advertising ratio
2. Recognition as a priority department requiring a detailed selling plan, advertising, merchandising, display, and signing
3. Weekly review of performance to expectations
4. Scheduled competition shops
5. Deliberate merchandising mix for ads (to secure full market potential)
6. Ad mix to establish leadership

Here again is an example of zeroing in on the important "sleeper" sales opportunities (with the exception of the expenditure limitation). The point to remember is that when "sick department" opportunities present a picture of 25 percent and more increases, you should of course, establish correct line-by-line goals. But you cannot expect the job to be done within the limited expenditures of the early (sick) sales budget. You will need new budgets, not only for advertising, but also for your inventory.

The clues for the sick exception and other "plus" sales opportunities always exist. The year-in-year-out process of improvement is never ending. Once opportunities are identified, the department manager will proceed to dig further, and when he or she does make a verbal commitment, you can bet it is one that is already "in the bag". You'll be able to tell by a manager's smile that a sleeper item or line or another source that will give the "plus" sales volume has been discovered.

The importance is the digging. The more you dig the more merchandising meat and magic your strategy will carry and the more productive your investment will be.

But . . . you still have too great an element of chance to feel assured your strategy will be effective. Though you may do a very efficient job of providing the clues and all of the necessary yardsticks to a department manager, not all will dig or respond all the time. The reasons are many, all of us being human, and it would take another book to cover the subject. You must, therefore, build concrete assurances that all of your *key departments for each specific promotional month* will in fact receive special attention and each *will* respond with meaningful sales goals.

The key department or lines for any given promotional month can be identified as a:

1. Top ranking and volume department
2. Top traffic department (transactions)
3. Department in its selling peak
4. Top profit department

You may have one or more in a category and the number of top departments or lines will depend on your store size and type. A department store, for example, in any given month, may have ten or twelve key departments. Taking proper care of these specific departments will afford you considerable safety and assure your powerhouse promotional punch.

There is one more assurance a large retailer should not pass up. When we develop our strategy in later chapters, we will propose, for the large store, a major store-wide seasonal event for two or three of our promotional months within a six-month season.

These events afford you a natural opportunity to assign sales quotas for the particular period, usually of a nine- or ten-day promotion. The quota to give each department is a 10 percent increase over last year's net sales for the similar period. The quota gives the same motivation as the sales goal, the department manager must dig for ways to capture the "plus" sales.

Goals alone are productive and meaningful; certainly a store is better off with them than without them. But, when you, as the strategist, can successfully promote initiative and resourcefulness in your merchandising people, you would be missing a great opportunity if you did not channel the individual energies strategically to good-of-total-store.

All are individual efforts, but all are part of your program. For example, you want to insist upon a sporting goods department goal commitment, and hardware, and paint department during the month of April; before or during your major event. You would want to insist upon goal commitments from every department for the specific month each department peaks in sales.

This is how goals are used—collectively.

CONCLUSION

We have touched on many major systems and stabilized many variables. Though many may feel these initial requirements would be better discussed after the exciting part, I felt doing so would be a grave deception. The most creative strategy will not work without the implicit base. Nor will it work without separating the two managing segments of your business.

You must also understand these chapters represent a basic presentation, purposely kept simple for clarity. There are, to be sure, many more complexities to retailing, but as we mentioned in the beginning of this section, ours is a trick, to gain knowledge and experience quickly by creating a model modestly sized. By managing the important, you will come to know what to do with the not-so-important; but remember that however unimportant the subsystems may appear, they cannot be dismissed.

We talked also about playing the winners, and the best months, but there are times, for specific businesses in traditionally slow months, that some dollars must be captured in order to exist. It is true that something should be done. My suggestion is not to coast or do nothing, but only to save your big investment for the time it will do the most good. Some dollars can be rightfully allocated to the slow period. But your strategy will be different then. Promotional ideas will be discussed in upcoming chapters, but, for example, consider a rug cleaning service. In a slow month, you no doubt have to give a markdown to your consumer as an incentive to buy. But you must also keep your costs down in this same period. It would therefore *not be prudent* to promote your low-end or lowest priced job, which may indeed be the most popular. The reason is that low-end price point items have a smaller margin to work with. You may have to have twenty customers or jobs to equal one large cleaning commitment. With a larger unit sale, you have a greater margin to work with—you can give a bigger reduction—and when compared to numerous small jobs, it will require less work. Your operating cost will be lower. In other words, in slow times promotion to create traffic (people) can be a very costly proposition. Few if any retailers are successful at it from a profit point of view. Review your big dollar volume producers and give a sizeable reduction for the rug cleaning of nine-room homes. A few of these transactions will get you by, and profitably. Slow times are also the period you will do much of your implicit planning. When the top selling times come your plan will be ready for your tactics, and you will have the money to act them out.

My message to those of you who are new to retailing is that there is much common sense to apply to your business other than what is presented in our model. You should, implicitly, do whatever needs doing in order to avoid crises and to maintain your ability to perform. You ought, however, to be very clever about it.

PART II
Intrinsic Strategy:
The Short-Range Tactical Plan

*If a man will begin with
certainties, he shall end
in doubts; but if he will
be content to begin with doubts,
he shall end in certainties.*
—Francis Bacon

8

TIME ON TARGET:

Media Tactics

The methodology for implicit strategy (the advance plan) is easily applicable to all store types and all sizes. But, for intrinsic strategy, the individual store's marketing activities and the tactics programmed for each *promotional month* present a considerably more complex and personal proposition because no two stores are ever exactly alike. Within any retailing category a store can be classified as one of four sizes, small (S), medium (M), large (L), or extra large (XL), and the departments or lines of goods each store carries can also be identified as S, M, L, or XL. Though we are only talking about four sizes, the combinations of department sizes existing with store sizes are unlimited. The XL store can have a small department and the small store an XL department. So it is worth repeating—no two stores are ever exactly alike. Broadness and depth of assortments that make up a line of merchandise for one store will always be different from its "similar" competitor. This unique mix and the different combination of marketing problems each "similar" business will have will create strategy differences. Therefore, no two strategies will ever be exactly the same, regardless of how alike two stores may seem to be.

The conclusion then is that the only true pre-planning input common to all retailers is the implicit strategy base—the six-month program of events constructed to the timetable of traditional retail selling opportunities. Intrinsic strategy is primarily a local task of communication. The message to be communicated to your potential customer is a representation of your unique inventory. Local advertising is a merchandising job of carefully crossing your "t's" and dotting the "i's". What all of this adds up to is that no competent outsider or book can create the firing-line strategy for you. Only the retailer can develop a comprehensive strategy that works. This strategy will consist of a potent advertising schedule for good-of-total-store and tactics *best suited* for promotion of the retailer's specific and unique enterprise.

Every retailer is indeed unique.

I cannot write an advertising schedule for you, nor can I recommend to you which media to use or when and how much; I can, however, give you insight to retailing's general strategy formulas and rules before the task is begun.

The first axiom to lock deep in your memory is your uniqueness. Its power is the lifeblood of your enterprise; it is the extension of your personality the consumer will remember. The first strategy requisite therefore is to determine exactly who you are and your reason for being. If you do this, then you will gain the natural ingredient necessary for meaningful retail advertising messages and effectiveness. This ingredient is called *USP—the unique selling proposition.*[8] USP can be recognized in the best of national manufacturers' advertisements. But for the manufacturer USP is applied to the individual product; for the retailer, the product is your store, your inventory mix. The manufacturer's aim is to create demand. The retailer's job is to announce "We have X brand now".

The magic then is not in the brick and mortar, nor is it your fixtures, layout, or services—though these may have some uniqueness, they are not the important substance that moves goods in and out of a store *quickly.* You cannot, of course, advertise your entire store. The task then has to be reduced to a strategic item representation, a unique mix, one that is timely and competitive. This is what you must communicate. The insights to be gained in this chapter deal

---

[8] Rosser Reeves, *Reality in Advertising* (New York: Knopf, 1961).

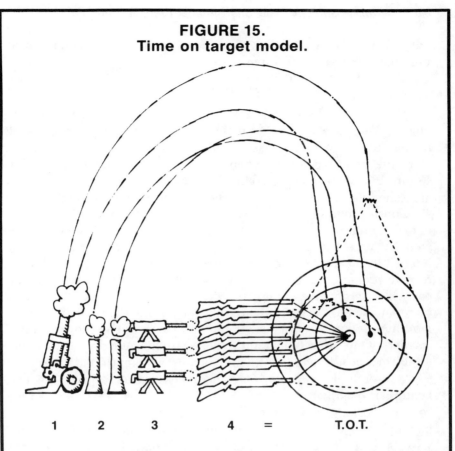

FIGURE 15.
Time on target model.

1   2   3   4 =   T.O.T.

Just as one cannot use a rifle to hit many numbers, your total campaign cannot consist of only "shotguns" or "cannons." Rifles are used for immediate hits, in the heat of the campaign. But there must be preparatory conditioning of the total objective. It is as easy as counting to four.

First, mass bombardment with general event shells before the sale days begin. Second, another event bombardment, but one of greater accuracy—and closer to the starting time with the specific market zeroed in. Third, the opening of the event is within even closer range, and there is a presentation of assortments—many items mixed with the feature and subfeature items, aimed at specific consumers.

The event continues with more rifles, new and specific items. This is the nucleus of a good campaign. In the first four days the battle is won or lost. The media mix used for the campaign will vary by store and according to the market conditions. The aim is the total realization of your market potential.

with media: the what, how, where, why, and when of communicating your mix to the consumer.

FIRST STEPS

Figure 16 tells us where and when implicit strategy planning begins. The proper place is in the store, by the people responsible for day-to-day sales, because all business is local. The proper time to start the planning job is when the six-month budget (point I in Figure 16) can be completed in adequate time to permit the advertising schedule to be written for the first promotional month of the six-month program. What may be adequate time for one store may not be for another. For example, after your six-month budget is finalized, the ad schedule for the first month of the season must be written, goods must be ordered and received. Some stores can order and receive promotional goods in a week's time; another store, generally part of a large chain, may require four to six weeks. This time factor must be calculated carefully, or the first month of the six-month period will be missed. It can and has happened to the best of retailers. Once this time requirement is determined, you can then establish a deadline for completion of your six-month budget.

Seasonal planning steps are relatively clear-cut, quite similar to headquarters advance planning, but with intrinsic programming, you are working with actual figures and *real* life-and-death, specific marketing conditions. You begin with department (or line of goods) sales budgets for each month of the six-month period. Chart their percentage of importance to the total season. Apply your departmental advertising ratio to the *total* seasonal budgeted sales to arrive at your departmental dollar advertising budget for the *season*. Next, spot your ad expenditures (a percentage of total season) to monthly sales patterns. This will give a monthly advertising expenditure starting guideline for each department. An overall view is taken and adjustments are made for good-of-total-store strategy. The end result will be a finalized advertising budget, for each of the six months, for all departments in the store. Sixty or thirty days before a month begins, you will finalize the store advertising schedule for that month. The schedule is then merchandised, ads prepared and released to media.

The task is that simple, procedurally. But intellectually, the strategist has much to consider. The first is the ability to have dollars

FIGURE 16.
Intrinsic strategy steps.

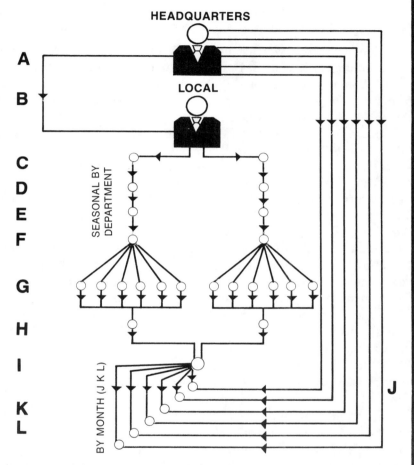

Intrinsic strategy begins with the local-store strategist (B), and ends with the merchandising of the store advertising schedule (L).

The steps generally followed are: (A) Headquarters six-month promotional calendar of events is released, (C) Departmental six-month sales budget is finalized, (D) Departmental seasonal advertising ratio to sales is determined, (E) Departmental seasonal dollars advertising budget is calculated, (F) Seasonal advertising dollars are allocated to departmental seasonal sales pattern by month, (G) Departmental advertising budget for each month is totaled, (H) Departmental month adjustments are made for good-of-total-store, (I) Total store six-month budget is finalized and program is adjusted to the headquarter program of events, (J) Monthly candidates for advertising are chosen, (K) Ad schedule for the month is written, (L) Ad schedule is merchandised.

to spend for advertising when the opportune time comes to spend them.

DEPARTMENT AD ADVERTISING RATIOS

If your store is worth having, it is worth advertising. A retailer must announce his wares. But all departments and all lines are different. Some are exceptional profit producers, others produce dollars in great volume, and others produce lower volume but more traffic (people). Some produce a combination of the three. It is to your advantage to recognize these differences and give higher advertising ratios to the "people" producing lines or departments and smaller advertising ratios to the larger dollar volume producers. Keep in mind that your concern is good-of-total-store. You give a higher ratio to a natural traffic department (i.e., housewares or domestics) not only for the good or need of that particular department, but also for the good of your total store. All departments cannot have high advertising ratios. It is important, therefore, to create a departmental "mix" in your strategy. To do this, you must first determine your department advertising ratios. How much should be spent for each department is a question only you can answer. A better question would be how much each department will need to do its specific job. One appliance store or department may get by with a 1.9 percent ratio to sales for advertising in one market while in another, the "like" store will require as high as 3 or 5 percent. When you are initially determining a ratio, keep in mind you are making the commitment for a season. The appliance department with a 1.9 percent ratio for the season may be allocated 3.0 for a specific month's advertising and 0.5 percent for others.

It is also of value to remember that advertising ratios you may learn about through other books or through associations, though they are valuable guides, are only averages and not always consistent. There are many points to consider. Some published ratios include a co-op advertising expenditure and others do not. For example, I know one store's published advertising percent for a specific department is 2.0 percent, but with co-op, it is actually 4.0 percent. If you follow the 2.0 lead of what advertising percentage to use, you will be at a competitive disadvantage. You must also remember that another store's co-op may be considerably different from yours. For many chains, co-op expenditures do not dictate the actual merchandising of items that the manufacturer's co-op plan would demand. These are factors you must consider if you desire your strategy to work effectively. You must study your market and your major competitors, particularly their ads. What is required for the season to get the job done is the point where you begin. It may be too high—then you must come up with the clever solution. The point is, the job is there—something has to be done—there is always an answer. You cannot drift.

We have mentioned several times that all items, all lines, all departments have selling peaks and ebbs. The task before you now, once you have determined your advertising ratio, is to know *exactly* when the selling peak begins and when it ends in *your own market for your specific departments or store*. You will want your placement of advertising dollars to gradually build up from the beginning of a projected "up" sales trend and peak the expenditure, very carefully, just before the sales peak, *cutting under it*. By carefully cutting under the sales peak, you will gain extra ad dollars you can use to push best selling goods just before their peak. These extra advertising dollars will give you a very important competitive edge. By allocating advertising dollars seasonally, you become a good-of-total-store banker, a planning broker.

The retailer is, indeed, working to exceed budgeted sales. This seasonal advertising allocation method does not increase risks, but instead reduces them. We know in what departments to place high expenditures and when. Now the media question can be considered.

How should media be used, when and why?

Media "real" home coverage, cost of media, and competition are the major factors that will influence your ratio decision. When your department ratios stand the test of several seasons, you will come to know the correct percentage for each of your departments or lines.

TIME ON TARGET STRATEGY

Not unlike other marketing propositions, media is a difficult subject to write about, because all media situations are different, even for those stores in the same category. The creation of a strategy common to all is impossible. Many factors influence a media decision. While one medium may work well for one store, it may not work for another. The competitive factor, the ability of media to cover the homes in your market, a new store location or an old store location, unlimited funds or restricted dollars, all contribute to the media decision. We can, however, get some semblance of a clear starting point by considering a common fallacy.

All of us have a general knowledge of radio, television, direct mail, transit advertising, and billboards. These, in retailing circles, are often referred to as supplemental media. The major medium is understood to be newspaper, and some 60 to 70 percent and more of large store advertising dollars are allocated to it. But very small stores will spend considerably less and possibly allocate 60 to 70 percent of their ad budget to a mix of other media. Because of the large dollars spent by the giant retailers, percentages can be deceiving, and also more often intimidating. Averages are fine for your own general information, or for comparing media totally to each other, but what will make up your final appropriation for media will be that which is specifically necessary to get your job done (achieving cash flow and hitting a near money target).

Your media interest is to reach your market, or a specific audience, for immediate results. For most retailers, the prime concern is home coverage in their market. Your advertising budget will present limited dollars for you to spend, and the home coverage you want will dictate the media you will use. There is no such thing as "a" major media. What may be major for one retail establishment may be supplemental for another store. What the retailer strategist tries to achieve month-in-month-out is a productive media "mix".

I have found the minimum home coverage requirement necessary to actually see results from my advertising effort is 60 percent. Below that figure, sales per dollar invested will decrease and your cost ratio to sales will increase. Above 60 percent home penetration there is a good chance your ad ratio will decrease.

To achieve a minimum of 60 percent home coverage, you need a media mix of great flexibility. Your advertising dollars must be free and not locked into frequency contracts or any other cost reduction gimmicks which are designed to commit you to a dollar expenditure for a month, or specific size ads for each month or each week. A popular newspaper contract to sign, once you have discovered the correct media for your store, and if there is an advantage in signing it, is a bulk rate contract. This contract is based on a total year expenditure commitment. You enjoy your earned rate as soon as you sign the contract, but can fulfill your commitment any time before the contract expires. If you spend more before the contract period

FIGURE 17.
The major media choice.

There is no such thing as **one** major medium as this photograph from the late 1930s illustrates. For some products, transit advertising was considered the major medium.

Even today, what you may determine as your major media in June may be your supplemental media for July. The strategist selects media for a specific purpose, for a precise time, and for a particular place to achieve a desired reaction. The choice is not a general one, regardless of how large or small the medium being considered may be. Nor is the choice one based on a personal preference or an isolated opinion.

Photograph courtesy of Transit Advertising Association, Washington, D.C.

ends, you will earn a lower contract rate, and the new rate applies to all the space in the contract year; the dollar difference is presented to you in a cash rebate. If you do not fulfill your contract, you will have a short-rate applied. The short-rate means you will have to pay the difference between what you have paid and the higher rate for the bulk space you actually used. Contracts have their advantages and discounts are important, but never at the price of sacrificing your flexibility.

Prudence with contracts is not an unkind statement against media, because I have experienced exceptional results from all media with many different types of contracts; but I am not in the media business, the flexibility requirement was never overlooked. Your concern is your store, your total store. Always: you want to move goods out of the store, and if one medium can't give the penetration to do it, then you must come up with sources that do. The media mix that gives you 60 percent plus home coverage in your market is the media to begin with. But it may not be the correct one. You may wish to change the mix somewhat. It is of great importance to always, I repeat, always remain flexible. Remember, media people truly want you to succeed, but they will not pay your bills for you if you have insufficient sales. The media decision is yours!

For intelligent use of media, first clearly *define your market—* whether it be by metro area or by strict neighborhood boundaries. This will give you input to put a fix on your coverage need, the numbers so you can measure to your 60 percent coverage requirement. Next, *understand who you are* (what type of store you want to be) and how many competitors there are in your market area. *Know your competitors* and what they do. But do not necessarily follow the media they use. There are all kinds of factors in retailing that make the combinations of competitive inputs impossible to list. These inputs are important to determine the size of the job to be done and how much money you will need. You must, of course, know your business, but regardless of what that business may be, all retailers must penetrate no less than 60 percent of the homes in their market to get results from investment.

The only way to judge whether your media mix is successful, after you have assured yourself you are reaching 60 percent of the homes, is by your cash register. You cannot play a waiting game; results have to be reasonably immediate for a retailer. By reasonable, I mean one to four days after the advertisement has been published.

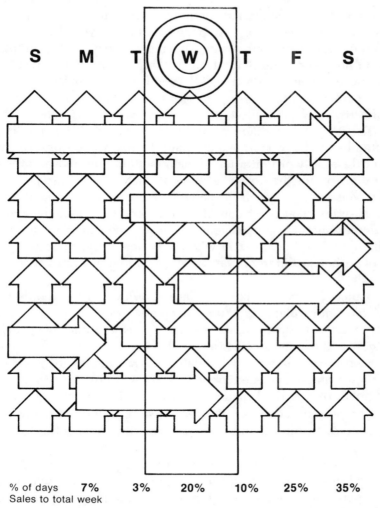

FIGURE 18.
The items job in media.

| % of days | 7% | 3% | 20% | 10% | 25% | 35% |

Sales to total week

Scheduling of advertisements for different days of the week (frequency) is one means of boosting your "real" home penetration. The creation of a media mix is another. But to realize full productivity from each of these methods will require deeper insights. Much depends on what ad runs when. The solution is found in your items. Some items have a natural "long interest" life, i.e., major appliances. Other items produce an immediate reaction, traffic items with a short response lifespan. When you come to know item characteristics, you simply fill in the schedule, strategically building up response to the peak selling days.

If we agree our media aim is home coverage (numbers) and that you are restricted to the dollars you have available, then it will be easier to determine what medium is right for you. If yours is a small store and the major newspaper does cover your little area, the cost may be out of your reach. You may be paying for circulation you do not need. The point I am making is that your inventory is your success, your "good-thing". If you have the *correct* media mix for 60 percent home coverage *for your market*, your advertising will be effective.

The idea of a media mix is not new. Since the 40s, I have used it constantly for large stores and small. The strategy question is not one of the ability or limitation of each medium, but more so the consideration of the habits of your consumers. In your peak selling times, you want to reach 60 percent or more of your market with your message. You must consider the general habits of people and use a combination of particular media to give them your message again, again, and again. You will say basically the same thing over and over, but in different ways. Figure 19 demonstrates this principle.

A media "mix" is relatively simple to develop but requires considerable initial planning. You must know, *before you select your media*, what you have to say (the key items and lines of goods you expect to sell during specific times). This knowledge, with insight of your consumers' habits, will influence your media decisions and determine your major media choice. You will not want to advertise yard goods during the broadcast of a football game.

Nor can you advertise your entire store, giving in-depth attention to all departments and lines of goods. But, as mentioned in earlier chapters, you can give attention to the important producers for any given month. Some guidance to the big producers may already be noted in your implicit headquarters plan. If lingerie will contribute 60 percent of your sales in June, you would not want to advertise this line in the sports section of your newspaper or during a baseball broadcast. Perhaps the contrast would work, but I certainly would not chance it. Your merchandise, then, and the amount of expenditures available to you, will determine the media when, how, and where. When you also consider that your big producers will change month to month and season to season, you will gain additional appreciation for the flexibility need. Figure 20 is an example of one means used to determine your important producers for a month.

FIGURE 19.
Say it again, Sam.

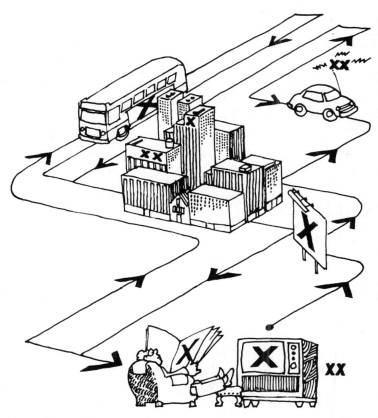

Unlike most national manufacturers' advertising investments a reasonable certainty of benefits for the retailer can be expected early on. If you consider the single purpose of retail advertising, to *announce* your "good thing," the requisite of reaching the consumer will become paramount.

Advertising for the retailer is not a single ad proposition, nor is it one of simple repetition. The key is to remember your consumer's memory box spills over—it retains very little of your "X" message. You have to communicate the same message over and over and over again, *but in different ways!*

If a retailer fully understands the habits of his consumers and the physical characteristics of his market, he can indeed engineer this proper media mix and should expect to reap immediate rewards . . . providing, of course, his "good thing" is, in fact, good.

FIGURE 20.
Department emphasis guide.

_____ 19 _____ **EMPHASIS GUIDE**
SEASON

DEPTS	FEB $	FEB ↑	FEB %	FEB ♟	FEB ⊙	MAR $	MAR ↑	MAR %	MAR ♟	MAR ⊙	APR $	APR ↑	APR %	APR ♟	APR ⊙	MAY $	MAY ↑	MAY %	MAY ♟	MAY ⊙	JUN $	JUN ↑	JUN %	JUN ♟	JUN ⊙	JUL $	JUL ↑	JUL %	JUL ♟	JUL ⊙
01				X		X					X																			
02																														
04	X	X																												
07			X																											
10																								X						
20																									X					
40																														
42	X					X																								
47																														
51																								X						
54							X																						X	
66																														
70																														X
71																														
72	X																													
77																													X	
78																				X				X						
90																														
91																														
94																														

$ Top dollar volume department
↑ Selling peak month
% Top profit department
♟ Top transaction department
⊙ Dominant item (line) promotion

It is strategically wise to promote the winners, and so it is prudent to identify them as far in advance of the promotional season as possible. Identifying dominant departments or lines for each month will lead you to these item winners. You can easily determine the winners by evaluating all the item candidates within a department for each month and seeing if they meet the five qualifiers above.

On a form similar to the one above, list all your departments. If a department meets one or more of the qualifiers, check it off under a particular month. This procedure can be followed for lines of goods if yours is a specialty store, and, of course, the qualifiers can be changed to conform to your specific retail category or service enterprise.

What you want from your media is not repetition, it is frequency. The only repetition necessary for your success is in your frequency of message, your company logo, address, store hours, and integrity in presenting your anticipations of what items the consumer wants, when they want them, in the right quantities, at the price they will pay and in the right place. The power of your message is your expertise in presenting and anticipating what the consumer needs.

Our conclusion then is that all media are good, but not always for you or the specific times you will want to use them. The success or failure of any media in my experience is directly related to what the retailer does with it.

There are two points to remember when you are developing your media mix: 1) *You* must develop the mix, not an outsider, and 2) All media have their standard rate cards, but there are retailers who have managed to write their own rate cards. In other words, if you have an original idea on how to use media, pursue it—you will find media people will be very pleased to work with you. You must also remember the Davids can get greater attention than the Goliaths. Because the Davids are not generally expected to do anything, they can actually steal, for little money, a medium for short periods.

You do not start toward a media choice by asking, "What does transit advertising have to offer me?" You begin by solving your problem. If you are a suburban store but 90 percent of the workers in your market work downtown, you will want to remind them of your major seasonal store-wide event. If most drive, then you will want an outside card, on the side of some buses, and some on the back, some on the front of other buses, depending on the direction of the bus at particular times and routes. The bus that travels through downtown 10:30 A.M. to 2 P.M. would call for a side outside card. The bus on the traffic way 3:30 P.M. to 6 P.M., leaving the downtown area, would call for an outside card on the back. I do not know if the transit people in your area can do this. But it is a question worth asking. It is a beginning to get what you want and need. If most of the people commute by bus, you would, of course, want an inside card. The idea is to make the media mix work to your specific strategic aims.

Direct mail can be an excellent medium for a small store if one consistently places himself in the consumer's shoes during the design of the direct piece. Put yourself in the position of the consumer from the time the envelope is first seen, then opened. Consider how the piece is folded and what the consumer sees first, the first words, the first sentence read, the proposition and the response required. With imagination, you can create outstanding printed pieces that cost you no more than similar unimaginative pieces. And it is important to remember media is not expensive for a retailer if it gets desired results. A $1,000 expenditure and a $10,000 sales result represents a 10 percent ratio to sales, a $500 expenditure for $5,000 in sales also represents a 10 percent ratio. The cost is valued by what you will achieve. A 2 percent advertising cost is certainly acceptable whether the dollars spent were $5,000 or $500. In other words, do not close your mind to what might seem a high cost. Investigate! Often, the higher media cost is the cheaper in a percentage ratio to sales achieved—that's why they demand more.

GENERAL KNOWLEDGE NEED

A retailer must have overview. He must know what is going on about him and in the industry. One very good source for marketing guidelines and input of this type is the *National Retail Merchants Association*. Your store may be in the specialty category and you will, of course, want to join a particular trade organization that represents your field. But you are also a retail store. To have an overview, you'll need to know the "goings-on" in the industry that will affect your business directly or indirectly. As a strategist, you will have to have some specific input on the general business of retailing. You must understand consumers have a limited number of dollars to spend each month. If they do not spend it on your wares, they will spend it elsewhere for other needs. It is therefore just as important to know when the consumer spends a purchasing dollar elsewhere as when the dollar is spent for your particular category of goods.

I do not mean to suggest membership to organizations is a mandatory requirement for your success. Many members of the finest associations file bankruptcy, just as non-members do. The point is that you are better off with it than without it. The difference is determined by how well you use the feedback these organizations make available to you. You must have norm figures to manage by. And in retailing, you largely manage to the exceptions; it is an enterprise of perpetual improvement. Because of this fact, it is of great value that you investigate the possibility of joining a trade organiza-

FIGURE 21.
A marketing tool—the planbook.

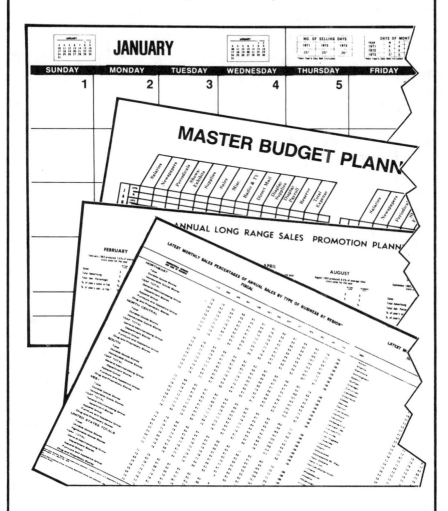

Illustrated are pages from an excellent retail marketing tool for both long-range and short-range planning and for recording results for next year's reference and guidance. The planbook is published annually by the National Retail Merchants Association and costs approximately $7 for members and $10 for non-members. This book features up-to-date statistics necessary for determining when the ducks will be flying for each individual retailing enterprise.

Courtesy of National Retail Merchants Association, 100 W. 31st St., N.Y., N.Y.

tion of your choice and also a general retail industry association that will fill your overview need.

RX CAMPAIGN MODEL

Though I cannot write a campaign schedule for your specific store, I believe it would be helpful, particularly for the readers who are new to retailing, to review a hypothetical campaign. The following example of a drug store is intended to introduce the thought processes and the volume of input necessary to make a campaign proposal meaningful. Campaigns begin only after considerable research is completed.

It is important that you have knowledge of your market and a true reading of your own establishment. Know the image your establishment projects. Are you offering a large selection of toilet goods and cosmetics? If not, the selection should be made up of the most wanted and requested brand items. Your displays should be attractively and conveniently arranged and the merchandise competitively priced.

Make sure the department of commercially packaged drugs is properly stocked. You should be carrying the best sellers such as vitamins, first aid supplies, etc. in the most popular sizes and brands. The consumer should be given individual assistance when needed in all areas: prescriptions, drugs, toiletries and fashion cosmetics.

Prescription department should be complete, so you can give the customer service at all times. It is frustrating for the consumer to be told the ingredients for his prescription are out of stock. The consumer expects the prescription to be filled when it is phoned in or brought into your store. If you have a delivery service, inform the consumer when the prescription is ordered.

Check reports of your ordering, reordering, stock, and sales patterns. Which departments are slack? The sick department problem is seldom an isolated case. Separate the store into departments or categories for advertising purposes.

Be aware of what is happening in the industry in general and your area in particular. Industry publications give information on present trends and can project the future marketing trends of prescription needs and drugs. You must have this information to proceed intelligently and to plan ahead.

Think of your consumer types—are they mainly the elderly, young, or all ages? The teenagers are a good target market. Women are traditionally the biggest purchasers of products in the drug industry. Teenagers are future parents who will be doing this purchasing for their families.

Your advertising should be directed toward your present market and the potential increased market you will be reaching.

One drug store I researched (part of a large chain) had primarily elderly people for customers. The manager consequently merchandised the store for this age bracket. The courtesy was even extended to ordering special brands of tobacco, toiletries, and other products for regular customers and holding the items for pickup. These were not large selling brands so the store did not normally stock them.

This kind of extended service might not be possible in each store within a chain. Your particular consumer market determines the type of advertising, merchandising, and service you should do.

My research verified the findings of various national drug surveys that indicated the desires of the consumer and problems facing the drug store industry.

The mainstay, drugs, is affected by the changes in the number of pharmacists in the industry. In recent years, the number of pharmacists has decreased considerably while the number of prescriptions has risen dramatically. Prescription business amounts to 50–70 percent of total business, pointing to the need for additional sales of toiletries and cosmetics and packaged drugs.

Knowing the pharmacist is not important, but knowing that the pharmacy service is competent and quality prescriptions and drugs are always available is important.

Often part of the answer to lagging sales problems is to revamp the total store image to reflect these consumer needs and then to communicate this store image better than before and better than your competitors.

Taking all this information into consideration will give you the overview needed to actually begin planning a promotional campaign.

The following proposal for improving slack sales in the prescription department includes this important total store and market overview. I have deliberately chosen a large drug chain's lagging prescription department as an example to give you more pieces to pick from.

Although your strategy is aimed at improving the RX department, there should be an additional tie-in program for toiletries and fashion cosmetics to increase store traffic. This is further explained in Figure 22.

It must be remembered when approaching RX promotion that special advertising laws exist for drugs and that stores must conform to the laws for their particular state.

The first step to take when instituting a promotional campaign is to design a six-month advertising calendar. For a successful RX promotion, start by charting the number of prescriptions filled, by market, each month. Figure percent of each month to total of six months. Guided by this RX pattern chart and taking into consideration major corporate events and calendar holidays, an ad schedule can be created. This schedule will vary from store to store within the chain—this is to ensure that your campaign will be geared to your particular consumer market.

During the six months that the campaign is to run, an internal bulletin, published monthly, should be circulated to keep involved personnel abreast of the campaign's development. This will help to promote new ideas and to foster in-store enthusiasm.

The key to effective advertising is to use every available opportunity to promote your store or department. With special packaging a customer can become your walking billboard. Consider adopting a special catch phrase or logo design—for example, "Another prescription filled at Jones Pharmacy", to be displayed wherever possible—on your shopping bags, wrapping paper, and labels. Choose a color combination and design that can be easily incorporated into your present store set-up. Everything from the color of twine and sealing tape you use to the paint job on the store delivery car should be coordinated to promote your store and make your products and services identifiable.

After coordinating in-store promotional efforts to boost RX department sales, outside media avenues should be explored.

When planning a print media ad campaign, have a schedule that builds up to specific sales peaks. Take into consideration timing and weather, both of which can affect sales. With an institutional ad series, the goal is to create an image of quality and reliability for the RX department and the store as a whole. To this end, back page ads for pre-prints are designed with a tie-in to special toiletries and fashion cosmetics. Prepare drop-in slugs for tabs and newspaper ads in advance. These should be made up in strips and units in a variety of

FIGURE 22.
Determining item candidates.

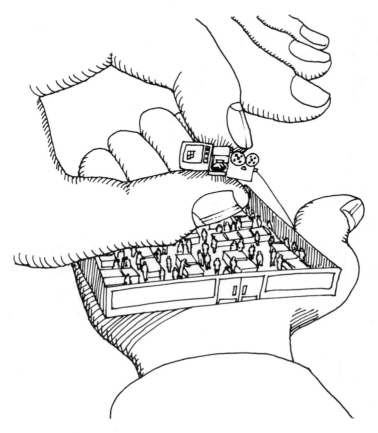

When a strategist has a department overview, he will never experience a shortage of item candidates for advertising. Departments are made up of lines, lines are made up of assortments, and assortments are made up of items. The consumer reviews assortments but buys by the item. The best items for advertising, therefore, are those that are part of your regular inventory and have sold exceptionally well with little or no advertising.

But the real trick is to come up with a mix. Each candidate should qualify as a people producer (traffic), dollar volume producer, or a super profit producer. Some will produce a combination of the three. The mix should be of items priced for low-income markets, for middle, or for high. The smart strategist will be certain that there is this mix to realize full market potential.

sizes—one column by three, two by three, four by six, in advance of publication.

Television and radio spots to be aired over the six-month period must also be prepared and scheduled in advance. Here again timing and weather factors must be considered and you will be stressing quality, integrity, and consistency. You might seek professional assistance in producing commercial video tapes to be aired on local TV. If your consumer market warrants it, be sure to direct spots to specific ethnic groups in your commercial.

Tapes for radio spots should be prepared with the same factors taken into consideration in your TV commercials. FM radio is as potentially profitable as AM radio and should not be overlooked when making up your radio campaign.

It is suggested that a basic approach is followed to establish yourself as a leader. To get off of program because of probes by competition is a mistake. Your competitors must follow you. When they do, the customer will then realize who the leader is, and your business will grow and grow.

Advertising is considerably more than layout and copy. The message is to use media to your specific need. But you must, when working with media, learn all you can possibly learn about each medium, their mechanics, deadlines, producers format, audience, philosophy, editorial contents, and how each is used by other retailers. The best way to gain insights into what media is all about is through media people. Make a tour of their offices, see their equipment, get up to date with what is and what is going to be. Learn about all of the media reports made available to retailers. Study the successful promotions recorded in each medium. Listen to suggestions on how to use each specific medium. You will come to know all you have to know about using each medium effectively and also be awakened to what is going on in your market.

Each medium has its own language. This should not intimidate you. The key words you will require for proper communication are easily learned. What you do not know, media people will be pleased to explain.

However, to keep media in its proper perspective and for your own general well-being, you must ask the questions. Do not depend on the media sales person to tell you all you need to know about media, regardless of how competent a salesperson may be. There is so much to tell! Ask questions! Questions provoke decision, and even

FIGURE 23.
The budget dilemma.

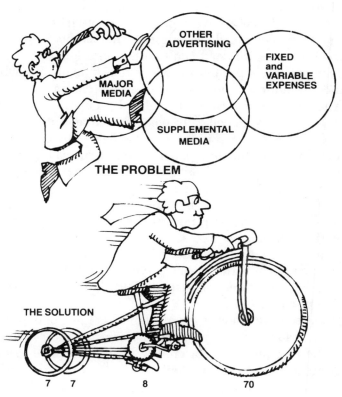

THE PROBLEM

THE SOLUTION

7   7   8   70

The problem illustrated above concerns the four major parts of the advertising budget. Unfortunately, many retailers have a difficult time controlling the budget. Often fixed and variable expenses will cut into dollars set aside for newspaper lineage or other media, or supplemental media will eat up any chance for dominance in a major media effort. Other times, no allowance is made at all for the fixed and variable expenses or for the cost of ad preparation.

The solution to this problem is to allocate a per cent minimum for each of the budget parts. Each requires dollars. A beginning point would be 70 per cent for major media, 7 per cent for supplemental media, 8 per cent for fixed and variable expenses and 7 per cent for "other" advertising. This leaves an additional 8 per cent to add to supplemental media if necessary or to use for other advertising. You will find these other minimums will generally hold up as sufficient to accomplish your tasks.

if busy, media salespeople will always spend the time to answer your questions. Questions that a retailer asks may be new to the salesperson who would never have thought to mention the fact you were after had you not asked the question. Remember that questions in search of answers will lead you to other questions.

Some of the important questions to ask involve four basic areas of concern: audience, production, cost, and contracts.

You want to know the audience and circulation within your marketing boundaries. Specifically what percentage of the homes does media cover? Media can give you these figures by census tract or by postal zones. Does the newspaper have any special zone edition that covers your specific market? Will they insert a pre-print in the papers for subscribers in your market?

You will want to know how much it will cost you to reach these numbers. This cost figure is necessary to make a meaningful comparison with other media choices.

You will want to see lineage reports and other media reports that tell you when various retailer types spend their advertising dollars. Are the advertisers consistent? Did they spend more this year than the previous year?

What contract choices are available? Is there one that gives flexibility and a lower than the "open" no-contract rate? Will my rebate earned be in cash or media credit? I would want it cash with no strings attached. You will undoubtedly put earned rebates back into media, but you will want the freedom to place the dollars when and where you wish.

What help will media give regarding the securing, planning, and processing of available cooperative advertising dollars? Is there a delayed billing for co-op monies I spend in media? Does the media handle co-op requirements immediately (the copies of the ad, certification of expenditures, etc.)?

What are the deadlines for copy? Will the media give free art, copy, or layout service? Are art prints free? Will media pick up original copy and deliver proofs? How much should I budget for a 30-second or 1-minute TV or radio spot? Will media produce the spots for me?

How much does it cost to sponsor an old movie? The old Flash Gordon series—how much?

There are of course, many questions you will add to this list, but the important point to remember is, *to learn about media, ask ques-*

tions the large advertiser will ask regardless of how small you may be. You will be amazed how this broad input will spark ideas.

Media is indeed important—but it is what you do with it that counts. As with any good salespeople, the media people know their product, and know it well, but they cannot be expected to tell you how to advertise. They can make general suggestions of course, but they are not the retailer, you are. You are the one that must develop the productive media mix.

*Prosperity is not without
many fears and dislikes,
and adversity is not
without comforts and hopes.*
— Francis Bacon

9

STRATAGEMS:

Decisions for Assurance

Don't fight competitors—outsmart them!

Stratagems, the kind we will present, are not trickery; they are carefully programmed maneuvers to protect your major promotional investment. *They are added on top of the major promotional program.* Your aim is to create assurance of a continuing ability to perform. Stratagems, in a sense, are truly defensive actions and should always be considered as such.

Retailers are perpetually vulnerable to outside factors. Weather, sudden economic changes, new marketing conditions, or competitor promotions may cause sales for one of your major efforts to fall considerably short of its expected mark. It is proper and right to put the bulk of your advertising investment in times you can reasonably expect the bulk of your sales. This represents your basic plan, but these times, within each month, are usually short, two- to four-day periods, a week or ten days. This leaves you a relatively large choice of other times for "mini-builder" extra efforts, opportunities to pick up "plus" sales—a 10 percent increase for one day, a 20 percent increase for another two-day effort, and a 30 percent increase for another special effort day. These will add up to a "plus" sales cushion, and if the major event exceeds expectations, these extra efforts will add dollars to your profit column. "Mini-cost" extra efforts are never wasted.

The idea in outsmarting your competitor is to get the spendable income back before he does.

But here we come face to face with our old problem again. Because there are so many types of retailers, and each retailer is unique, the ideas proposed to you should only be accepted as thought starters. You should never do something that is a contradiction of your image, one you have built over the years. It is the intention of the author that you only review the ideas, pick out what you like, then adapt each to your own specific enterprise. You'll probably find that with this open-minded approach, your ideas, when finalized, will have no resemblance to the original that sparked it.

The point to keep in mind is that all retailers face uncontrollable forces and your dollar investment in advertising is one of pure net profit dollars. To which we might add, they are unearned, based on sales to come. *Your base program is therefore worth protecting.*

Although every new employee goes through an orientation class, mine in advertising was unusual. At an early age, I learned to pay attention to the basics, the natural retail selling opportunities, and extra selling efforts. My apprenticeship was at the headquarters office of a large chain, in the retail sales department (national advertising department), but in a very unique specialty unit within it. The sole function of this unit was to handle special requests from stores in the field. You might compare its function to the role of an advertising agency. Most of the chain's stores could not afford an advertising staff to prepare special efforts, or create special programs which would include, in addition to all prep, writing the ad schedule and merchandising the special ads. It was a clever conception. By using this department for special requests, the normal function of the retail sales department, that of providing the monthly promotional materials to stores, was not disturbed. The specialty unit was a very busy department. There were many different-sized stores to serve the very small, small, medium, large and extra large units, and the requests came from all—ranging from a "local sale" heading mat, art work for a special local buy, to huge grand-opening events. And also, during a certain period, there were many store closings we handled.

Later, I came to realize that we were filling requests for "plus" sales efforts—those in addition to the regular corporate-company

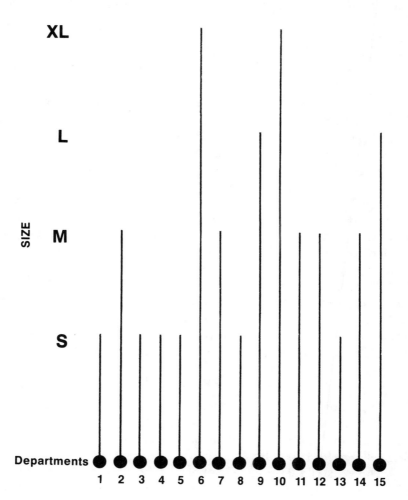

FIGURE 24.
The unlikeness of stores.

The Velocity Factor

Your friendly competitor may give outward appearances of being very much alike, but in truth every store has its own dominant line or department mix. The store profile given above indicates a velocity force of four dominant departments. Your profile may indicate one or five. When the specific dominance mix is recognized, in your competitors as well as yourself, and religiously programmed as the driving velocity force behind your advertising strategies, you can increase your normal good-of-total-store success expectations.

wide promotional program. I also learned the very best events that lend themselves to "plus" sales exceptionally well are grand openings, store anniversary sales, and store closings. The next in productivity, but not necessarily consistently, are warehouse sales, seasonal store-wide majors, and January/July clearances. Special selling efforts will always add considerable dollar volume to these events.

Following this group are the monthly store-wide majors.

The most productive tool or ad to cash in on natural "plus" sales opportunities is one that will always pay its own way, the store-wide omnibus ad for a one- or two-day promotional effort.

After these, you have the "extra efforts" group—the "mini-building" extra effort promotions that cost little money.

The "mini-builder" is different. It is not totally like your regular promotions. Its success, of course, can be found in the merchandise proposition, but its driving force is enthusiasm. Enthusiasm is needed for all promotional events, particularly your seasonal store-wide major, but it can succeed without "total" enthusiasm, the "mini-builder" cannot. *The "mini-builder" is a vehicle for a high intensity, a total enthusiastic personal selling effort in a very short period of time.* And it is also important to remember the "minis" are scheduled on top of the regular promotional program. They are local store initiatives. They are minor efforts, not the major one.

EXTRA EFFORT DAYS

This effort is an excellent means of securing "plus" dollars.

The following event relates to big ticket departments, but can be adapted to any business that maintains a "lead" file. It is an outside selling effort to close leads.

The cost of this event is a beer party, with pretzels, popcorn, and sandwiches, plus prize money or a special award for actual sales achieved.

The idea is to announce to your salespeople early in the month, let's assume March 1, that "super effort days" (or outside selling days) will be March 28 and 29. The promotion is one to close leads and on those days (personnel properly scheduled for some floor coverage), the salespeople are to go out to the consumer's home. It should be stated that their normal daily sales, comparable to last year, are expected (otherwise, the salespeople will hold sales; they still will, but some sandbagging is the excitement tool for you).

FIGURE 25.
Natural related department groupings.

NATURAL GROUPINGS

One of the very best tools available to a strategist are forms and reports that are organized by related departments (or line) groupings. The strategist will use these in planning and analysis. For example, if the home furnishings group represents 7 per cent of the store's expected sales in the month of February, he will give special attention to that *group.* His first thought is to the group. How much money does the *group* have for advertising? How important is the group? With group ad dollars, though each department will eventually be scheduled for its rightful share of the total, the strategist can begin with a campaign approach for good-of-total-store. He can strategically do more with a group accumulation of 3½ newspaper pages or 1,000 radio spots than he can with individual token expenditures. The first steps to be taken are group-by-group spotting of expenditures on the promotional calendar, then allocation of space departmentally within each group. A sampling of related departmental groupings is shown below.

Home Furnishings Group
- Furniture
- Domestics
- Gifts
- Floor coverings
- Bedding
- Housewares

Modernization
- Paint
- Hardware
- Wallpaper
- Plumbing
- Building materials
- Custom cabinets

Appliances Group
- Sewing machines, vacuums
- Refrigeration
- Freezers
- Laundry equipment
- Stoves

Apparel Group
- Women's sportswear
- Shoes
- Dresses
- Robes
- Lingerie
- Hosiery
- Accessories
- Men's clothing
- Boys' clothing

For each of the two nights, set up a "report-in" room away from the store—maybe a shopping center room that is generally rented out for a small sum. Set up the beer barrel, etc., and all the trimmings—signs, slogans, costumes, etc. For each night, have a "report-in" time, i.e., 6 till 8 the first night, 6 till 10 the second night. Divide your salespeople into teams. Have team prizes and individual prizes, and special awards for 50 percent quota makers the first night. If an unexpected sum is posted by some individuals the first night, the others will work harder the next night. All will, of course, hold their punch for the last night. Have a large board and post the reported sales as each salesperson checks in. Do this with much excitement. This approach affords you the opportunity to create some "loud" spirited challenges.

You must also try to have many people present at the event, other than the salespeople. You can accomplish this by giving other employees (non-sales) *small tasks* to do. The more small tasks, the more people—but each, as small as the task may be, must be acknowledged as a responsibility: Keep popcorn dishes filled. Suggest a song. All must be programmed. You want excitement, you want to develop a competitive spirit between the different salespeople or departments. This promotion is usually good twice a year, once for spring and once for fall. They will grow each year, but the temptation you will have to fight off is to schedule more.

ONE AND FEW OF A KIND SALE

This event is a sure winner once a year. It is made up of a long listing of many items. It can be communicated by direct mail or newspaper. The ad is a line listing with a montage of general illustrations, simply to identify the groups of goods offered. At the top of each listing, place this identifying heading. A sample item listing might be:

TABLE 9-1.
Example of a line listing ad.

QUANTITY	ITEM	WAS	NOW
3 only	13.5 cu. ft. refrigerator. Small dent on side/door.	$359	$188
2 only	19-inch color TV. Anonymous name. Scratch on side.	$289	$128
11 only	Women's warm-up suits. Slightly soiled. Sizes S-M-L	$ 34	$ 19

If you have many departments, you could group them. This promotion lasts best for one day or two. In your direct mail piece or newspaper ad, give great emphasis to the time your store doors will open. The event is great for big tickets, but small items, if many are available, also add flavor, store traffic, and excitement.

PREVIEW SALE

If you have a customer list or credit list, you can cash in with extra effort by extending these people first pickings of your super major or special event. The night before the event begins, extend them an invitation by letter. If they are legal in your state, prizes or lucky number discounts help to produce traffic for this one night. It is only productive, however, with a major event your customers already know is one of your best.

TEASER ADS

A teaser ad is often beneficial to the super major seasonal store-wide event. It is used when this event is scheduled during a highly seasonal selling time. Its obvious purpose is to build up excitement and attention to your event, but the real reason is to reduce consumer purchases in other "similar" establishments before your sale begins. The teaser ad message is very brief. Your logo must be easily seen and recognized and the ad's message simple.

	JONES
logo	DAYS

Starts Wednesday 9 A.M.

The ad starts small and increases in numbers throughout the newspaper's different sections (or number of times in other media) up to the day your full advertising impact is scheduled. If your sale begins Wednesday, Sunday's paper may have three ads, Monday's newspaper three, Tuesday's six. Artwork can be used effectively if it is simple, uncomplicated, and tied into your message. An example would be a woman's head (smiling) and a bird whispering into her ear.

THE UNEXPECTED

A store represents a marketplace—therefore, it should be exciting.

A store is exciting when it programs the unexpected, the new!

Your store is a stage. Your cast is your merchandise. And there are star performers you will play up at specific times, but, in addition, you will need a variety of special acts *that are not necessarily announced.* The idea is that when a consumer visits your store, it should be an exciting experience. The excitement is in the consumer's reviewing your assortments, their "just-looking", and this is when you hit them with the unexpected. They may not buy the particular item, but they will enjoy their visit, they will be back, and they will talk.

What are the unexpected special purchases? The items not normally carried in your inventory. Some of these items you may, after a favorable history of sales, want to keep in your inventory. But as a special purchase, your only purpose is excitement.

These are items you get in to and out of quickly. An example would be the TV video games. The market is certainly limited for these games, but they would have been exciting in your appliance department when they first came out. It would do you little good to have one or two after the games have become well known.

People like to browse in a store; but they want it to be exciting. An extreme example of a store that programs the unexpected successfully is Neiman Marcus. You must remember, however, the "unexpected" is only part of your program, a minor part . . . do not let it lead you to other paths. You will make great discoveries, tempting discoveries, but if you do sell an elephant, I would not reorder. You must develop a policy concerning this area and stick to it, though a time may come when others may work hard to convince you to do otherwise. And the unexpected must be related to your lines—an unusual ski jacket, an unusual drill, an unusual toy, an unusual game, a sampling of interesting things you cannot profitably carry month-in-month-out.

COMPETITOR DOMINANCE

Competitor dominance, by a store like your own, can hurt your major effort and therefore should not be tolerated for any length of time. If, however, a competitor's action is a promotional effort going against the stream, opposing retailing's traditional selling timetable, wish them well, because their life will be short. There are also times, associated with a specific sales event, when you can do little about competitor dominance. Certain sales, built by a competitor over many years, cannot be bucked. The best is to concede and, if you must, run along with them, cashing in on the extra traffic generated by their above normal expenditure. The old "Sears Days" event would be a fine example. But for some reason, Sears reduced this event handle to a whisper, and it has lost its year-to-year memory recall. Other stores have built up outstanding once-a-year anniversary sales. Months of hard labor are put into these events and there is no means I know of to weaken their dominance.

You should, however, if their peak selling time is also your prime time, strive to increase your own degree of dominance. In this case, consider first what you are up against. What, exactly, will your competitor do? When you learn this, then you can proceed to do it better, but not necessarily the same way. The question you want answered is how much they will spend for advertising. Next, how much of the advertising expenditure is co-op dollars. It is fairly easy to recognize co-op efforts in their previous year's advertisements. Will they use pre-printed newspaper sections or circulars? If the store is a chain, you can bet the pre-prints are a co-op or subsidized proposition. The bigger the chain, the greater the subsidy will be. One chain may charge the store $54 per thousand while another, and for a better pre-print, may charge $3 or $4 per thousand. If the decision to run a pre-print is local, you can be fairly accurate in assuming the store is paying a very low price. If the price was not low enough, your competitor would tell their headquarters buying office to keep the pre-print. The buying office is not interested in selling circulars to the store, they want to spread goods to the store, and all of the items in the circular have to be ordered to back up the pre-print. Another hidden factor, with chains, is that much of their co-op advertising cannot be identified. They receive manufacturer co-op dollar credits in cost of goods, however the co-op money is still returned in the price of the goods to the consumer; these dollars are placed in departmental funds. At prime selling times, when the headquarters buying department wants the store to advertise its department, the co-op fund dollars are made available to stores. Not unlike the dollars an independent store would receive from a wholesaler or manufacturer, the chain store agreement may be to pay 100 percent of the ad cost, or 75 or 50 percent. The big difference is that the independent must, of course, advertise certain items, dictated by the wholesaler or manufacturer. *The chain store co-op dollars are for the department's expenditure—the store merchandises its own local ad.* This is a very important difference and places the independent at a distinct disadvantage. The independent can reduce the disadvantage if he also secures his co-op credits in cost of goods and proceeds to create his own departmental or line co-op fund. Whether the manufacturer or the retailer merchandises the ad, the consumer pays for it. All you are doing is seeking merchandising freedom by collecting the monies and putting them into your own account.

Co-op monies are pure net profit dollars, and if you have a fund, there will come a time you may be tempted to transfer the cash to your net profit column. I do not know if this is legal, but I do know if you do so, you will be defeating the purpose of the fund. Its purpose is to give you extra advertising dominance when you need it.

The reason it is important to know how much your competitor is spending, and how much represents a real expenditure to correct sales, is that they may be following a path with great risks that will lead to ultimate disaster. If a store is dominant but they are spending 7 percent of sales for advertising each month with no co-op, you would certainly not elect to follow them. But many tricks are used to get big dollars for the big promotions. Sometimes a store paying a higher rate than it has earned will have its newspaper contract expire in the month of the big promotion. The rebate can amount to thousands of dollars. Their advertising expenditure may add up to 5 percent plus, but their real net figure may be considerably less. Do not be misled.

The dominance key to study then is co-op dollars. The more dollars that have no merchandising strings attached, other than a department or line, the more competitive your competitor will be. The more co-op dollars he has, the more lineage he will have, or expenditures in other media. There are five types of advertisements: omnibus, line, departmental, related item, and single item. And there are five types of promotions: omnibus, major store-wide, seasonal major store-wide, departmental, line and related item. If you can identify the type of events your competitor uses and the type of ads, you will come to know his strengths and weaknesses. If he is using all omnibus ads or an unidentifiable ad type, his dominance will be easy to overwhelm with your own mix of ads, for less money. If your competitor has all of his eggs in one basket, a huge pre-print or many pages on one day, you can beat him again. The reason is that people do not read their newspapers every day. You can, therefore, be more dominant than he is, except for that one day, but you will be reaching more homes. How many people read their newspapers in a day? My rule of thumb for easy arithmetic and to provide a cushion for my possible merchandising weaknesses is 50 percent. The actual figure may be slightly higher, possible 56 percent.

If I spend the equivalent of six pages of advertising in one day, in a newspaper with 300,000 home circulation which is representative of 60 percent home coverage, I will, in fact, be reaching only 150,000 homes, or 30 percent home coverage, far below my requirement. But if I ran one page Wednesday, two Thursday, and three Friday, I would be considerably closer to hitting the total 60 percent home coverage I need, and in addition, I would have dominance two days out of three. For the same money.

The strategy to accomplish this, for the best productive outcome, is your ad mix. If we keep our competitor in mind and we remember the purpose of advertising is only to announce your anticipation of consumer needs (your inventory), we can get some clues on what to do. Much depends on the season; this will tell us what our strong departments or lines are. Items from these are what you will communicate. *The objective is synergy of ads—each is deliberately planned for a specific role.* The ads are not merchandised individually, but as a group. In other words, you are really developing an item campaign. And of course the items you offer should be proven winners or non-basics you believe will be winners.

The message is to study a competitor's dominance. When you do, you will usually find you can do something about it.

DIVERSIONS

While it is true traditional retail selling opportunities remain unchanged year after year, it is important, promotionally, to refrain from following one advertising pattern to the letter, even if it was successful, for two reasons. First, the times and marketplace conditions always change, and second, if it were feasible to remain pat, your competition could beat you at your game.

There is a diversion tactic in retailing strategy, but the required changes of strategy come quite naturally if you are alert to the new times and conditions versus the same period last year. You will make changes in your media mix and your ad mix; however, the changes are not made for sake of change but are ways to do a better job. With this flexibility, your competitors will never be able to pinpoint your up-coming strategies. You do not follow them. They follow you. You are not concerned with beating competition, you are "the" competition!

SHOCK TACTICS

There are times to wake up your market. A change of pace is necessary.

One way to do this is to deviate from your normal graphics (not your logo) and merchandising approach. Your decision regarding a merchandising change will be based upon your competitive position and prevailing conditions. For example, if a discounter is eating into your share of the market and yours is a general merchandise store, your special merchandise approach could be to emphasize all low-end goods. But have a good excuse for the "shock" presentation.

Remember that in no way should your "shock" campaign read or appear as an attack on your discounter competitor; any inference he is taking business away from you is free advertising for him. The excuse is your creativity, your graphics, a change of pace, an exaggeration. If normally your ads are 40 percent illustration and 60 percent copy, you would go 90 percent art and 10 percent copy. If normally line art is used for illustrations, going all photographs would do the trick. All you need is a good event (excuse for the special effort) and this temporary cross-exaggeration will enhance your leadership.

PAYDAYS

Before charge cards, noting paydays on his planning notes was extremely important to the retailer. Whether or not this importance exists today is a question worth exploring. The present era seems to be one in which people want to clear themselves of debt. They'll spend when they get the cash. If this is true, you will want to spend more advertising dollars at that time, you will want to know the payday of the major industries in your community.

CHANGE OF CALENDAR

In early chapters, we emphasized how important it is for a retailer to operate on monthly budgets and pre-determined sales expectations in order to control our cash flow aim. Without adequate cash flow a retailer would miss the majority of the traditional retail sales opportunities for his lines of goods or departments. Accounting systems seldom overlook a month that has one less Saturday this year versus last year. But, strange as it may seem, the error is not so rare in advertising.

If you had four Saturdays for June last year, and this year you have five, you could feel safe your last year's figures will be met for that month, and you should expect to meet your budgeted increase. If the opposite were true, you would, of course, have a more difficult time. But a retailer cannot remain stagnant, he must grow, he must always beat last year's figures. Exceptions, of course, would be major catastrophies. You can always beat last year, because a Saturday lost can be picked up if the loss is noted at the time you are writing your ad schedule. The number of Saturdays, Mondays, and other days for each month changes year to year. It is important they are noted.

Holidays change. Many fall on different days of the week than they did last year. This will mean a sales plus or a minus. Some years the holidays will fall to give you a natural excuse for a strong week-end (four-day) promotion. In other years, the holiday will pop up on your worst selling days of the week. The slack must be made up. The answer is to program extra selling efforts . . . early!

Of all the "mini-cost" extra efforts we reviewed, my favorite is "the unexpected": The reason is that with it, everything else works better . . . it provides continuing, on-going excitement.

Do not let the smallest opportunity for "plus" sales pass you by . . . because if you do, that opportunity can never be recaptured; it is lost forever.

There is no great and no small
To the Soul that maketh all:
And where it cometh, all things are;
And it cometh everywhere.
—Ralph Waldo Emerson

10

ADVERTISING STYLE:
The Differences
of Store Classifications
and the Difference It Makes

Advertising is a necessity for all of retailing, whatever variety a store may be and wherever it may be located in the world. But the general retailing and advertising strategy that works well for the one retailing category will not always work as effectively for another store classification. Whether it be a chain or an independent, a supermart, a general merchandise store, a restaurant, catalog showroom store, discounter, drug store, department store, or specialty store, each store has its own marketing characteristics and its own problems that affect its advertising style. A general knowledge of *all retailer advertising styles* will influence and add valuable scope to your own strategy. It would be prudent for you to gain insight as to exactly what the style differences are and why, and particularly their limitations.

For a restaurant, the very best and most productive medium of announcement is the satisfied customer word-of-mouth advertising. Recognizing its effectiveness, the restaurant owner will quite naturally direct his attention and advertising dollars toward the promotion of word-of-mouth advertising. Unfortunately, as we mentioned in previous chapters, while we can identify a general business classification, any two stores within a particular category are never exactly alike. Their problems will be the same, but because conditions and circumstances vary, each will have its own combination of problems resulting in different retail approaches and different logic. Keeping this in mind, one's review of style will be a general overview of each category, emphasizing only their major differences.

The following explanations of the different retail types are based on my own experiences, and are my own opinions. These are given to provoke questions, your own questions that must be asked pertaining to your particular store. Some may spark an idea—others may be thoughts you are well aware of. *The point is, we are after the important overview.* After thoughtful analysis of your situation, you will be better prepared to apply strategy to your advertising effort.

THE SUPERMART

The largest of all retailing is done by the supermarts. Most are parts of regional or national chains with central buying and central advertising (headquarters controlled). There are great pressures in retail advertising, but none are as great as the last-minute merchandising and pricing of weekly ads of the supermart. The weekly ad is their major and most important effort. The most popular ad days are Wednesday or Thursday, and the most scheduled ad size is facing pages or double trucks (center spread using the inside margins or gutter). Of the grocery ads, 99.9 percent are scheduled for the grocery section, the newspaper section that consumers traditionally single out and immediately look to for weekly grocery specials.

Today's supermart, not unlike other retailers, is voicing increased concern for the future due to the inability to see some clues as to precisely what it may be. Will there be fewer stores, or will an overstored situation persist? Will there be shortages? How will computers affect operating costs? Will there be a food crisis? Will inflation continue? Will the supermart carry more general merchandise lines? Will eating habits change? Will supermarts be locally merchandised? What will the advertising approach be? Will there be more institutional advertising? Where will the future co-op dollars be placed, will more manufacturers promote directly to the consumer?

In addition to a justified and serious concern for the answers about the future that allow a retailer to plan, many may also be

FIGURE 26.
Know your market.

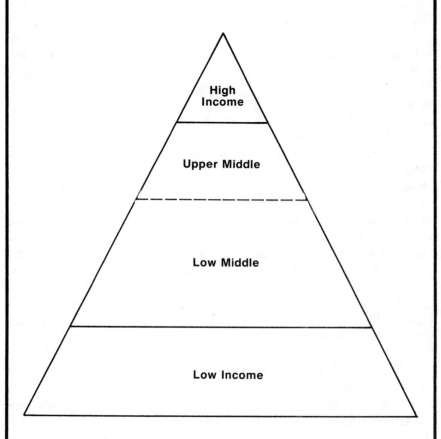

High Income

Upper Middle

Low Middle

Low Income

The Market Pyramid

All people have needs and demands but these are not always the same. Even the basics have price point and quality differences. It is equally important to know who are you after and who your competitor is after. Your store must reflect the needs and demands of your particular consumer and your advertising must consistently reflect your store's merchandising philosophy. If you do not, more often than not you will miss part of your market. If you persistently merchandise your advertising by one specific price point, low, middle, or high, your store will eventually be thought of in that image.

facing a present dilemma of depressed sales, rising prices, and very unhappy consumers.

Regardless of what the economy may be, the supermart depends on a steady stream of customers, week-in-week-out. When customer traffic diminishes, the ability to maintain goods at fair prices will become difficult if not impossible. Realizing the need for weekly traffic, the supermart manager will usually increase the promotion of his specials, in numbers or with deeper price reductions. The supermart may induce their customers to return, but in order to support the price reductions, it must raise the price on other goods. The result is, very quickly, the consumer returns for the specials only. The supermart manager has a dilemma.

To solve this type of problem, many of today's supermarts are deliberately, or with no other choice for survival, approaching merchandising of their food goods the way a general merchandise store merchandises its items. Unfortunately for the supermart, at least for the time being, this merchandising approach seems highly questionable for two reasons. One is that the supermart could never hope to maintain the high average markup on total inventory of 40 or 41 percent necessary for a promotional merchandise mix of good, better, and best. There are some experts who believe this is the future, that the day of low margin food prices is gone. This remains to be seen. However, today the merchandising approach is a dangerous one. Supermarts are trying to force a solution to their problems onto the consumer, but the consumer does not seem to be buying it.

The second reason is the basic precept that the supermart must be priced right, total store, every day of the week, because people buy their groceries by the week. I think we can also agree that consumers would like very much to buy all of their grocery items in one store. To engage in the general merchandise store markup mix means (if it were possible to accomplish) the supermart would also have to register its important volume of a month's business during a specific event of eight or nine days. And, like the general merchandise stores, they will have to plan and be satisfied to secure the bulk of a year's profits and business in just two or three months. For the supermart management which believes it can settle for this, I would have to believe they can also expect some small and alert fellow to take care of the consumer's weekly needs. Because retailing is not the same from category to category, retailers cannot change their retailing style to correct a depressed sales predicament. Consumer buying habits and patterns are very distinct for each retailer, which is why the different retail types exist.

Whatever direction the supermart may elect to pursue or whatever changes the industry must endure, it would appear nearly impossible for the supermart to follow the merchandising principles of the general merchandise stores.

It is obvious, at least for the present, the style of effective advertising for a successful supermart is one that supports the supermart's low everyday prices, day-in-day-out, and will not be able to compete seriously with other store categories. The supermart, like the restaurant, is extremely dependent on satisfied customers who will spread the word. The store must be priced right, across the board, every item, and if it is, its parking lot will always be crowded. The volume needed to maintain low margins will become a reality. Promotion will help, but the supermart should not place the cart before the horse hoping to capture volume through promotion and advertising. *Promotion only accelerates the sales of a good thing and advertising only announces the good things.* Both cost money, and they cannot create miracles; they do not and cannot create the good thing.

The supermart that wishes to change by pricing the total store correctly can build or regain volume in a short time because it does not have the one major advertising problem other retailers have, namely readership of newspaper ads. Wednesday or Thursday grocery ads are the most highly read pages of any newspaper. Having this vehicle, the supermart can present a fine assortment of specials. But the total store must be priced right, when the people visit the store, or again, only the specials will sell.

Every retailer has the opportunity to solve his sales problem without going to a new concept or gimmick. The problem is usually one of desperation, of not meeting important prerequisites of organization, of a lack of methods and procedures necessary for discovery and development. For example, an opportunity that warrants a deeper look are the toilet goods items, also called health and beauty aids—the sleeper line of the supermart. Would it be better to treat health and beauty aids as an individual department? Considerable research ought to determine what lines will be carried, what items, what price points. A store must have its promotional items to accelerate sales, but with a strategy to promote the sales of "that" department, not the total grocery store. In other words, would it be better for the health and beauty aids department to have its own profit and loss statement? Should it continue to be used as a source of loss leaders to promote groceries? It seems to me to be feasible to demand that equations be applied to all items as to their profit productivity, sales volume productivity, and traffic (people producing) productivity, on a department basis, with a department manager who is responsible for sales of "that" department. Then the question should be asked whether it is truly impossible to make the merchandising responsibility a local one. The basic goods (assortments) to carry are best determined centrally, but the merchandising of advertising space and planning just might be 30 or 50 percent more productive if it were a local decision. These are only questions. Whatever the questions and whatever the answers may be, they all effect style and strategy for better or worse.

Merchandising, pricing, and promotion have changed, but the style of supermart advertising has remained the same for many, many years. The breakdown of their advertising dollar has changed little:

Newspapers	.690
Television	.130
Radio	.080
Direct mail	.095
All other	.005
Total[9]	$1.00

The approximate percentage breakdown of advertising space is basically the same as years past, excepting the increase in HBA:

Meat	31.5
Produce	13.5
Dairy	7.5
Dry groceries	39.0
HBA, non-foods	8.5
Total[9]	100.0%

It would seem, as it has for the past twenty years, the newspaper will remain the major medium for the supermart because of its high readership. However, it should be noted many supermarts have effectively supplemented their newspaper effort with TV and radio.

---

[9] Source: Newspaper Advertising Bureau.

Milgram's of Kansas City is one fine example. Today, it would seem the supermart advertising style, regardless of media used or new attention (desperation?) to health and beauty aids, is one of weekly announcement. Its success will be in volume selling of food.

DISCOUNT STORES

The discount store, a general merchandise establishment, mass merchandises limited assortments. The discounter came into being by taking a page out of the promotional chain store book at a very opportune time. They promoted goods, originally many national and known big-ticket brands, at new low prices to sell in tonnage quantities. They broke the maintained manufacturer's list price. The combination of selling single items in large quantities and low overhead permitted a lower markup on the goods.

As the discounter firmly established himself on the retailing scene, many sophisticated chains with the good, better, best merchandising approach began to devote most of their attention to selling higher markup, top-of-the-line goods. The department stores accordingly pursued the sale of still higher priced goods and never did learn how to price and sell appliances. The action of both store types opened the door for discounters to become, for a relatively long period of time, the fastest growing retail stores in America. They, of course, could not endure forever.

Most discount stores lease the majority of their departmental space to independent operators. Many of the licensees have departments in two or more discount chains at the same time. There are exceptions, Venture stores being one. Venture stores refer to themselves as discounters, but are closer in truth to being a promotional chain. Assortments at Venture are by no means limited to a sampling of a line of goods, and most or all departments in Venture are their own. K-Mart also refers to themselves as discounters, but I have to suspect they are a variation of Sears' principles. Their methods and systems have to be considerably more sophisticated than one is lead to believe. Other discount stores have restricted themselves to one dominant line of goods; furniture is one example. At the discount store the consumer took with him anything he bought. If he could not carry the item, he would be obliged to arrange his own delivery. Contrary to the conventional chain store and the department store, the discounter did not rely heavily on major promotional events. This was very likely not a matter of choice but more a weakness or lack of internal sales promotion methods and systems. There were exceptions, again Venture being one. Most discount chains are believers in central advertising and merchandise each month's advertising space schedules through a series of quarterly or monthly departmental licensee meetings or by mailing a notification of the scheduled space to the licensee. Discounter advertising planning, execution, and media selection methods only remotely resemble those of the sophisticated department store and the conventional chain.

Originally, the real discounter was not a merchant in the true sense of the word. He deliberately did not merchandise an item mix to produce departmental overall satisfactory markup and turns. He did, of course, merchandise, but he was after key unit sales and volume tonnage item sales. The promotional strategy used to bring customers in zeroed in on national brand wanted items, often reduced to near cost or cost and sold until they stopped selling. There was great excitement and a ready market in the early days and eventually this excitement, plus their ever increasing numbers, led management to push again and again for more and more and lower and lower sale priced items from its licensees. As the number and amount of promotional markdowns increased, licensees increased their departmental markup on total inventory goods. Eventually the percentage of advertised item sales at cost or below to total departmental sales grew to high, dangerous proportions, forcing the licensees to balk. The overall store pricing gradually increased and became the same or close enough to the same as that of the traditional chain, but the discounter did not have the consumer services, total store "mix" expertise, or the methods to promote and maintain balanced sales and inventories. The discounter began losing its customers. The licensee/management relationship to promotional advertising became one of playing management games —one side pushing for more promotional markdowns, the other taking a firm position for survival. Some very professional acting took place on both sides of the conference table. Unfortunately for the licensee, the total merchandise expertise of the sophisticated chain or the department stores was not generally present in the discount management circles, particularly in the areas of promotional merchandising and advertising. They were heavy in financial expertise.

From the late '60s to the middle '70s, many discounters and

many licensees failed. Overexpansion, overstocking, a depressed economy, lack of merchandising organization, and a tired concept, all combined to threaten the well-being of the largest discount operators and the most prestigious licensees. But the discounter advocate, whether licensee or corporation management, has learned much from the many successes and hardships of the licensee/management experiences.

The sophisticated chains (Sears[10] among them) and the department stores learned something too; they learned not to give up their low-end goods.

While the discounter concept has many interesting insights that merit pursuit, it seems the discounter has yet to determine its own sales promotion and advertising approach, or exactly who they are. Venture always had a sophisticated approach and Woolco, it is evident, is developing one, and there are other discounters changing for the better. But the majority have an obviously incomplete ad program. Strategy is missing. Media selections are highly restrictive and often appear to be limited to personal preferences and not fact. The greatest obstacle to implementation of strategy is the considerable emphasis placed on pre-prints that force store coverage and ordering of a large number of items. This, of course, is very good for the printer of the pre-print and it is considerably easier for the centralized buyer or merchandiser to spread goods to the stores. (Centralized buying is good but centralized spreading of goods is in truth headquarters controlled merchandising.) The local discount store manager acts as the advertising manager, however this advertising function and responsibility is generally, and erroneously, limited to the checking of ads as received from the home office for release to the local newspaper. It would be very good to question whether this policy is the best one. Certainly the manager's time could be better spent than in this basic time-consuming function. In addition, in the retail industry advertising budgeted dollars are not exclusively for media. Advertising payroll is a part of the advertising budget. To deduct payroll exclusively for the home office advertising department reduces the local store's rightful share of advertising. The important question is, which policy would better afford the opportunity to increase sales?

---

[10] "Choosing a Chairman at Sears, Back to Basics," *Chicago Sun Times*, November 1977.

The inability to allow merchandising flexibility at the local level is also a serious handicap for the discount chain. In addition, for the discounter with many licensees, the problem of coordinated advertising strategy is accepted (mistakenly) as a near impossibility. "They" are different, it is said. As different as a licensee-operated store may be in the minds of the discount executives and their associates, the consumer does not see the difference from a traditional store and cares less. Is it too abstract to consider that success for the discounter would require systems and methods, forward seasonal advertising, strategy planning, and a strategic merchandising mix just as much as it does for the traditional chain store or independent?

The discounter's concept of low overhead is a good one, therefore it may be opportune to have certain requirements and yardsticks, but not necessarily totally the same as the traditional chain's. But there is another handicap popular in discount circles. It involves changing business conditions. Discounting is a boom economy baby. One of the problems of many discounters, or so it seems to this writer, is they are guided by well-meaning investors who are financial managers, not merchants who are more apt to adjust to trends. The capable credit executive, banker, lawyer, financial genius, tax expert, auditor, operator, though professional and competent in their own fields, cannot seriously hope to help solve the retailer's daily merchandising problems, all of which eventually affect his inventory position and ability to perform. *The failure to solve daily merchandising problems can lead a retailer to the brink of disaster.* Not unlike many of the retailer types, the discounters, it appears, lack the generalist. But this void hurts *them* more.

Like any other retailer, in the absence of a boom economy, the discounter who wishes to be successful will have to have merchandising responsibility and authority fixed (though limited) to where it belongs, on the local merchant. Though the local merchant, being department manager, store manager, or advertising manager, may be earning considerably less money than the non-merchandising investment executives, we have to ask if personal income criteria should be the real yardstick for authoritative evaluation of retail merchandising judgment and expertise. And, of course, the discounter has the additional problem of the licensee.

It seems the successful advertising style for the discounter ought to be basically the same as the promotional chain, centralization with decentralization and perhaps with an exciting touch of the department store which would, of course, be a distinct advantage. This can be done. The discount stores have been having their troubles, but they have much to consider; there is an answer to their dilemma and when they find it—they may very well be the major force to contend with . . . again!

RESTAURANTS

There are all types and sizes of restaurants and to write "the" advertising style for restaurants would be a serious error. But everyone would agree the prime requisite for success of a restaurant is good service, good food, good drink, and a congenial proprietor. The mixture of these four, at a price the consumer will pay, is the magical mix that will have the consumer coming back again and again. It promotes priceless word-of-mouth advertising.

If the restaurant has these requisites, all the proprietor has to do is keep reaching out and meeting new people. He will do that by being active in the community or by advertising through various media.

Advertising for the restaurant is not for the purpose of selling the spaghetti dinner to old customers, but for securing new customers. But the best means for securing new customers and holding most of the old is word-of-mouth advertising. A bottle of wine sent to a table (part of the advertising budget) does much to convey the message that you appreciate the customer's patronage. It also adds excitement. Or "Try this pie, let me know how you like it." If your advertising budget is $400 for the month, that is equivalent to many bottles of wine and pieces of pie. The point is, if a restaurant owner is aware of his real objective, the advertising strategy will very likely produce desired results.

How can a potential new customer be led to a restaurant?

Special prices will not do it; we are assuming the restaurant prices are fair already. With a special price, you will be suspected of hurting in sales, and if you are hurting, you are not that good; maybe you were, but you are not now. At least that is what the customer will think. And if you continually promote the special "plate" or price, the consumer will always expect it.

Depending on the newspaper's layout, it would be good to advertise on the theater, society, or sports page. But publicity is more important. After the local pro team beats the arch rival, possibly you could arrange a photo of a local couple celebrating with a dinner at your restaurant.

Pictures, publicity, pictures, publicity, and more pictures are important for the restaurant, particularly if the pictures are of personalities, husbands and wives, who are in the current news. The photos should *always* include the proprietor and an interesting view of the restaurant. In addition to major newspapers, there are many magazines and neighborhood papers that welcome timely and interesting photos.

Radio ads during morning commuting time would also be a valuable expenditure.

Each restaurant has its own pattern of big nights and slower nights. The radio schedule should be determined by the sales pattern.

Would you advertise the night before your big night, two nights before, or the morning of? What works best in one market will not always hold true for another. The morning driving time of the best night would be the first logical choice.

What is the big date night in your market?

In Chicago, it is Wednesday night, other than the weekend.

Drive-in restaurants, dinner clubs, and others, each must also reach out to their market, each must do the required research to determine when and how to reach the desired market.

For the drive-in or fast food market, the name must become a household word. Children are your best helpers—children, TV, and occasional coupons. The kids always want to go out to eat, but the coupon gives them help, a reason to force a favorable decision and immediate action.

Important for all restaurants looking for more customers is to become involved in local school affairs. Go to the school fathers' and mothers' club meetings, preferably the mothers' club. Offer to cook a fund-raising dinner in the school, donate the food and have the school supply the volunteers. Or just donate money when the need is meaningful. For your worthy effort, you will be rewarded with many friends and new customers.

Restaurants, not unlike the general merchandise stores, must make an advance plan, execute it, and measure results of the overall performance (by the cash register). Not unlike the general merchandise stores, the restaurant must work very hard to retain old customers and continually gain new ones. The restaurant advertising style is unique, a highly personal one.

DEPARTMENT STORES

Fortress of the sleeping merchant prince!

There is one major difference between the chain's general merchandise store and the true department store. The department store has buyer department managers and the chain store does not. Department managers within the local chain store do not generally buy goods, they order goods to a pre-determined merchandise assortment and promotional item offerings sent to them by the corporate buying office. This difference makes the truly sophisticated department store (of which there are few) the most exciting marketplace in town. The department store activity is heavily pointed toward women and what's "new" can be on the counters as much as a year ahead of the traditional chain store. The department store buyer will also, in addition to buying direct from sources of supply, purchase goods through a buying syndicate or office. There are some restrictions placed by the buying syndicate, but the department store buyer will continue to have more merchandising flexibility and freedom than his major competitors, the chain store department manager and merchandise manager.

The advertising procedures explained in my book, *Retail Advertising: A Management Approach*,[11] take one exception with the department store. The department store advertising/sales promotion manager is still the planner and the policeman of advertising expenditures, however he will allocate considerable amounts of advertising dollars to the buyer department managers for scheduling their own ads. This does not mean the department store has less forward planning requirements (that is a myth or cop-out); the visible difference will be that the department store will have a greater number of individual ads. The department store, with its many large volume departments, many being over one million in annual sales volume, does not become overly concerned with the total store advertising schedule and the grouping of limited inches for maximum impact (though we can wonder what would happen if they did).

Though I was born and raised in the chain, I have always believed the department store should be the innovative leader, of all the various retail establishment types. They have many advantages and are in an envious position. If anyone can discover new sources for goods and take immediate action, it is the department store.

---

[11] (New York: Lebhar-Friedman, 1976).

But today, any retail trainee will acknowledge the facts that consumers have no loyalties, all of the old service and convenience "pluses" of the department store are also available at the sophisticated chain, and many are considerably better than the department store's. This means that regardless of store type, anticipation of consumer *needs* will be tomorrow's major factor for success.

It would be wrong for the department store to adopt the total promotional approach of the chain (100 percent central buying); however, it would be advantageous for the chain to adopt many of the approaches of the department store, which they have already done. The great events, the fantastic item promotions, the super exciting assortments, the new—this is department store style . . . or was—and for everyday folks, not exclusively the upper third of the market pyramid. Now the chains do it. And department store advertising impact—its thunder—what happened to it? I suspect strategy is missing. It would be good to ask why the struggling prestigious department store has not looked deeply into the methods of the lowly Sears, the world's most successful retailer. By that I mean, it certainly is time our department stores looked at Sears' methods, particularly replenishment and seasonal coverages, the distribution centers, the policy, the disciplines. A London retailer, the most successful in Europe today, did just that in 1926.

There is no problem with advertising a going department store, because you have the big dollars to do it. It would then seem that their systems and methods are weak, which in turn makes advertising erratic and weak. The discounters, if the department store people are not too proud, also have some valuable experiences for the department store.

In my opinion, the super department store is the store of tomorrow. They will be made up of many leased departments, but there will be a true strategist at the promotional controls.

On stage, Merchant Prince . . .

CATALOG SHOWROOM STORES

There are general merchandise full-line catalog showroom stores and there are those that are limited catalog showroom stores. The "limited" group catalog generally offers jewelry, gift, camera, small electrical appliances, and sporting goods, while other catalogs represent full general merchandise. The catalog showroom store has been around for a good many years, as long as or longer than the discounter. First Distributors in Chicago is one example. However the general popularity of the catalog showroom did not increase until the jewelry licensee of the discounter and discounter management had to look to more profitable means to move his goods for income. The "Hey, let's open a catalog showroom store" became a popular and welcomed suggestion.

The catalogs are very expensive to print and very few individual retailers would be able to afford one exclusively, if any at all. A committee or group is formed, generally of six or ten different retailers, each from different markets across the country. They merchandise the catalog, usually working with an individual called a catalog coordinator, then each commits for its desired quantity of books, resulting in a total press run that will bring the cost of each catalog to a price the individual retailer can afford. Cost may run to 67¢ each, or 74¢, and often times higher. Quantities of books required for each of the six retailers may range from 5,000 to 50,000 or more. Prices are controlled to keep most retailers' prices consistent, and merchandise changes are restricted or not allowed at all. If allowed, the individual retailer pays for the change. Only the covers and a few front, middle, or back pages carry the individual logo of the retailer and his exclusive message. The catalog coordinator, usually associated with the printer, works with the committee of six retailers and finalizes the pages which eventually go to the printer. The group actually merchandises the book with a considerable amount of "as is" manufacturer camera-ready art and full-color transparencies to keep costs down.

The store is structured to display a sample of the most wanted catalog items. The back-up stock of each item is stored in an area behind the showroom. The customer looks over the displayed goods or the catalog, then orders the item wanted from the catalog desk. Sears Roebuck had been doing this long before discounters arrived on the scene. The only difference is that Sears pulls the goods from their mail-order warehouse. But, in truth, so do the catalog showroom stores, if you visualize wholesalers and manufacturers being their warehouse source. The idea that each catalog showroom store has large quantities backing up each item in their catalog is very hard to accept. Few, if any, of the members of the merchandising group would have the money for such a large and slow turning inventory. Having the money or not, only the best selling items are given a meaningful back-up stock. The prices of the non-jewelry items are generally very competitive and while goods are shown for display purposes only, the one exception is jewelry. This is where the limited catalog showroom store makes its markup. All the dressing of the showroom is a sampling of goods to produce traffic (more potential customers for jewelry). The jewelry section of the showroom store is a very complete and professional department.

The general full-line merchandise showroom catalog store is larger and it combines the discounter function, with goods out in some quantity for floor sales, with use of the catalog for many other items the store cannot stock in quantity. It is a clever means of broadening their assortments with little inconvenience to the consumer and less inventory risk and investment.

Both the limited and the full-line general merchandise catalog showrooms spend little for advertising other than their very expensive catalog. A specific catalog showroom advertising style, other than the catalog mailed to select lists, appears to be nonexistent.

The catalog is highly questionable as being sufficient, promotionally; we ought to consider the obvious fact—it offers no merchandising flexibility. The catalog showroom concept poses many questions to be answered.

SPECIALTY SHOPS

A specialty shop might be likened to a department within a department store that has decided to go out on its own, "standing free" so to speak. It is usually family operated and provides a good means of living by meeting a highly select merchandise need of its immediate community. The specialty shop's major advertising effort, largely direct mail, is limited to holidays, Christmas, and possibly one major effort in spring and fall.

The local newspaper, ad agency, or a freelance advertising person will prepare their advertising, or if the individual proprietors have writing and art abilities, they will prepare their own ads.

The same merchandising principles of item mix and advertising strategy apply to the specialty shop as to any other retailer.

The specialty shop, however, is selective. Most of them are exceedingly careful not to restrict their market too much by persistently promoting one price point, low, or middle, or high. Some can effectively sell exclusively high price points, but their numbers are small. This type of store takes a great amount of merchandising expertise.

Radio advertising works very well for the specialty store, as do periodic mailings that are not totally restricted to customers, but also reach out to new corners of the market with each mailing. Prizes are productive with the mailings, but the most productive of all are the seasonal markdown sales. If the markdowns are taken courageously (they usually are), the store can become famous through the "best" kind of advertising—word-of-mouth.

The specialty shop's advantage over other retailers is its personal service and attention to each consumer and his selection. Being buyers, the specialty store merchants can be more up-to-the-minute in meeting consumer needs, particularly in fashions. And where the specialty store may have two or three of a dress number, the chain would have twelve and the department store eight.

The advertising style for the specialty store is different from the chain or department store's. *Its best advertising is word-of-mouth and its own direct mail list, but it must also continually work to reach new customers.* The message of what the store is must be continually presented; however, when you have one or two of everything, it is difficult to advertise these items without considerable problems, not to mention the productivity these items must have to warrant the advertising expenditure. This specialty store problem is generally accepted by the consumer. The advertised item usually only represents a portion of a line.

But, like the department in a department store, the specialty store must have a pre-determined advertising ratio to be applied to budgeted sales. The old rule applies—if the store is worth having, it is worth advertising. But here the similarity to a department store may end. The women's department in a department store has other departments that produce traffic for it. The specialty store does not. The specialty store, with its limited "total store" funds, must approach advertising planning as the ad manager would for the total general merchandise store.

The specialty store advertising percentage to dollar sales ratio is considerably higher than a similar department in a department store, and the dollars are not generally allocated to item and line selling peaks each month. The dollars are generally concentrated on the very major events that occur during peak selling periods. The specialty store can and ought to develop strategy.

Though their advertising style is different, the philosophy of shooting the ducks when they are flying is also the distinct philosophy of the astute specialty store manager. Their "ducks," though, fly earlier than the norm.

DRUG STORES

If there are any retailers who face a very difficult future, I have to believe it would be the super drug (variety) store combination. The threat will not be in additional numbers of drug chains, but the supermart. If the supermarts ever learn what merchandising is all about, they could seriously trouble the drug store; health and beauty aids lines is one example of opportunity for growth and profits, profits generally not afforded the supermart.

It would seem the style for the drug store is one comparable to the supermart's. The drug store is not a department store nor is it a general merchandise store of a promotional chain. It cannot for long promote in the style of the department store or the general merchandise promotional chain. Its structure, merchandise assortments, and people restrict the drug store or chain to the requisites of the supermart, everyday low or fair total store pricing. The drug store will make the best of natural selling peaks for specific lines of goods, but eventually must have week-in-week-out traffic and volume. It must consistently sell items other than the specials advertised.

It should be noted, and many will claim, that there are and have been many drug chains dealing in general merchandise who were seemingly successful as promoters. But it is not until one looks deep into the times, organization, co-op income, procedures, and methods that a suspicion is aroused as to what the real degree of success was. The successes are often ones of personality, a concept, or gimmick, not of a common way of doing things—norms another store could easily duplicate.

It would seem the drug store category also has its share of questions to be asked. But unless success characteristics change dramatically, it would appear the drug store advertising style will remain one of week-to-week persistency.

THE GENERAL MERCHANDISE CHAIN

It might be best, right off, to identify the general merchandise chain as a sale house, a promotional institution. At least, Ward, Sears, Penney, and others like them are. And we can add K-Mart to the list. Their corporate eyes are first fixed on the natural selling patterns and sales peaks of each of their departments. From that point a promotional calendar of events is established, goods are bought and offered to their stores for each of the specific events. They stock and sell what the consumer wants.

The routine business of keeping the stores stocked is a separate and distinct function. This is a very important point to keep in mind, however it would take another volume to explain all of the requirements pertinent to this everyday function. To determine advertising style, it will be sufficient to understand that the promotional arm of the general merchandise chain has its own individual reason for being.

The general concept of the promotional chain is to move goods to and through their stores, quickly. It is a total concept with the centralized promotional arm as the means to accelerate the movement of goods, with discipline, to a preconceived timetable. The events, corporately programmed, are mandatory for all stores; however, the promotional goods offered by each buying department are subject to the local store's own judgment and the local store determines the quantity to be ordered.

By a review of this very brief outline, one can begin to understand that the chain store advertising style is corporately initiated and reflects a corporate strategy. All ads and ad materials are prepared nationally for each of the promotional months and cover all of the items offered to the stores.

If a store has the flexibility to order its own specific items and quantity, then there must be a flexibility in the corporate advertising service received. For example, a store would not want a dominant illustration of an item it had ordered very few of; a smaller size should be available.

If the corporate program was sufficient to meet all needs, then all "similar" stores in the chain would realize about the same sales per square foot of selling space. This does not happen.

The advertising style of the local chain store, it would seem, is one of corporate strategy influence complemented by local innovations and promotional merchandising expertise that is opportune and familiar to the store's local market.

Every merchant within each of the categories discussed, I am sure, can add many identifying and meaningful characteristics to this chapter that are common to his particular retailing type. The important point made is to alert the reader to the fact that there are differences between the advertising approaches for each store category. Successful advertising ideas for one group are not always successful for another. Know who you are and know your differences. These differences determine style, which will in turn lead the retailer to the strategy decisions best suited to his particular store.

What I must do is
all that concerns me,
Not what people think.
                                        —Ralph Waldo Emerson

11

How the Strategist Thinks

Paul Smith* gave up a successful corporate career of many years standing to pursue the fun of doing, which he said no longer existed for him in the company where he was employed. If you count by years, Paul is near fifty. He is a cost analysis engineer. He has an analytical, scientific mind. Whatever he does, he wants to do well, to the best of his ability, in the logical, natural, and correct way it should be done. He is well educated. He has several masters degrees. Two years ago, with zero retailing experience, he opened his own bookstore, and contrary to popular failure expectations, he has proved the experts wrong. Today, by any measurement, Paul's bookstore is a solid success.

Paul is typical of many new entrepreneurs with a corporate background. But how does this unlikely merchant, a small neighborhood inexperienced retailer, continue to achieve above average success while others like him are pushed to the brink of disaster? And when we reflect on the conditions of today's marketplace, we have to agree with the experts, or at least suspect, that business failure will

---

* The name is fictitious.

be a certainty for nine of ten new enterprises. Is the success of this little bookstore a fluke?

Paul could be lucky, but there is one fact I found I could not easily dismiss; he is not alone. There are other success stories like his own, and many more in the making. It seems the interesting question to pursue is not what factors surround the new successes, but instead what common personal characteristics of the inexperienced group that succeeds set them apart from the inexperienced retailing group that fails.

In each of the retailing strategy seminars I have conducted for people new to retailing, the ages of the participants consistently ranged from twenty-two to the middle fifties. Two-thirds of the class was over forty, and of this group, almost all had masters degrees. One or three of each group had a Ph.D. Each of these individuals came from different corporate backgrounds, and all were interested in how to advertise a retail enterprise. Better than two-thirds of each class was already engaged in their new business and the others were contemplating the move. All came as infants—listeners—and as non-conformists.

They had one aim in attending my seminar, the experience input—not necessarily to learn what they should do or how to do it, but to gain quick insight to what has been done. They were putting their private ideas and what they had already learned from other sources to a test. This is characteristic of a strategist, and you can believe when any strategy choice is to be made, it will be their own. Each of these individuals shared the belief that the only true security is what one provides for himself. They therefore quite naturally follow the idea that any power they might have will be in their own personal, individual ability to perform. They are their own stars. They are not cowards. They will take risks.

But these character similarities of the new successful retailers I have come in contact with are not sufficient proof the new successful entrepreneur is any different than our grandfathers, the spirited and successful retailers of yesterday. And also, the new retailers who fail today often have the same characteristics. There is, however, one notable difference.

The successful retailers seem to have a distinct advantage—they don't know any better. They never had the image of yesterday's retailer. Society is not erratic to them, *it is simply the way it is*. These people are no wiser than grandfather or the struggling old

FIGURE 27.
Intellectual overview.

OVERVIEW

Retailing is a science, and the quicker a merchant accepts this fact, the sooner he will have his ship in order and his course charted. Any knowledgeable retailer can forecast an increase in small independent shops, but these new entrepreneurs, to be successful, will have to do their homework well. Their task will be considerably more intellectual than their grandfathers'. There will have to be a meaningful overview of the pertinent internal, external factors for effective decision-taking.

INTERNAL	EXTERNAL	JUDGMENT
ANALYSIS	**OBSERVATION**	
—Financial limitations	—Trends	—Market
—Resources	—Political	—Media
—Synergy	—Social	—Environment
—Strengths	—Technological	—Consumer
—Weaknesses		—Technical
		—Cash flow
		—Protection
	ANALYSIS —Forecasting	—Priorities
	—Sales patterns	—Buying
	—Surveys	—Liquidation
	—Competition	
	—Opportunities	
	—Studies	
	—Norms	

pro. Their advantage is that overview comes quite naturally to them. They are naturally aware of what is going on about them internationally, even though their enterprise, like grandfather's, may be confined to a neighborhood. These people are well aware that differences between social classes are disappearing; clothing is similar, everyone has the same mass media. They know there is nothing special about owning a car, any car. And whether the individual represents a neighborhood one-person enterprise or has corporate manager responsibility, each will insist upon analysis, observation, and judgment of internal and external factors. All of this comes quite naturally to these new, inexperienced, successful retailers.

They know very well inflation will affect them, that it is difficult to control and the profit lifespan of more products will be considerably shorter. They understand that domestic inflation means simply that many people are getting more money than their contribution to society is worth. They accept the social conflict as "normal times" and understand how it trumpets many changes. They therefore avoid being pushed into a corner by outside forces. They know, beyond a question of a doubt, they must be strategically flexible.

They do not follow—they lead. They take personal risks and be-lieve in fair value for contribution. They think the way to increase real income is by increasing productivity with competitiveness, creativity, innovation, and good-will. They do not believe you should borrow when you need money, but instead when it is oppor-tune to borrow. These new success entrepreneurs, with no retailing experience, subconsciously know all these things, because they were brought up in an erratic, ever changing, highly technological society. They were educated in it. They are natural strategists.

The conclusion is that, in the marketing era we are now enter-ing, only the strategist will experience a long success in an age of creativity, innovation, and personality.

Because strategists have been rare in our financially managed, technological age, it would be a phenomenon if the initial scratch-ings of so many would be limited to one city. The same, I have to believe, must be happening in other areas across our land and hope-fully, in other countries of the world.

If indeed, ours is a new age and the strategist is tomorrow's winner, it would be of some value to remember what makes him tick:

- He is a generalist.
- He has a sense of observation and analysis.
- He has the ability to synthesize.
- He is committed.

These qualities are not taught in any classroom, because a gen-eralist becomes what he is through natural inclination, experience, and self-teaching. One possible helping factor may be job rotation, but this does not always work. One can learn to be receptive to new ideas, but it takes more; being a generalist is a state of mind. The strategist is creative, an "Obvious Adams", an originator with confi-dence and the determination to see his ideas through, all quite natu-rally. He is not a conformist, because that would be a contradiction to his integrity, the knowledge that all markets change, and that strategies need a spark to ignite new life from season to season.

He has ability and looks far ahead.

His superiority is more intellectual than physical.

The new entrepreneur will have to be a strategist, because he will have to meet the need of great daring and personal confidence.

A strategist is a person of ideas, but these are basic general ideas, not vagrant thoughts. The strategist has a disinterested attitude and a personal submission to higher ideals—the constant incentive is to cultivate better selves. Tavel calls them the twenty-first-century leaders of people who will become leaders—true modern knights who look ahead and see clearly. This I believe.

They prove out Emerson's thesis: " . . . write better books, preach better sermons, and make better mousetraps and though your house is in the woods, the world will beat a path to your door."

The strategist will have immense determination and great originality. He wants success for the company more than he wants it for himself. Because of this devotion, he will be very demanding of himself and of others. His greatest satisfaction is intellectual interest in his work, in the knowledge he is accomplishing a task of decisive importance, contributing to and cooperating with others.

There is another quality about the new entrepreneur worth noting. He is indeed an individual, a free spirit of the first order, but he will talk to people, if only to clarify his thoughts.

Tavel, in his book *The Third Industrial Age*, covered this need from the consultant's role. What is said of the consultant's input can also apply to executives within the strategist's company. The problem is: times and conditions change, and a history of success can be detrimental to a company's future well-being. The tendency has always been to follow successful patterns; however, in our new age, these must be constantly challenged with timely, pertinent questions. There must be debate. But when all is said and done, the strategist will still be the individual who makes the decision.

Strategists want to be proved right. There will be a number of occasions when a strategist will get an independent opinion to be able to say he is reviewing or studying the matter, even though he has no intention of taking action. Tavel also tells us this.

The strategist, of course, must have authority over staff and line people. He is an advertising dollar banker, a planning broker for good-of-total-store.

He is a communicator. He possesses a vast store of knowledge, a wider view than the specialist's, though he has made his mark in at least one specialty, because he must know how the specialists think.

As a strategist, our new retailer knows creative snythesis does draw on cooperation of many people, but it has to originate in the brain of one man. Responsibility is individual by nature.

FIGURE 28.
The magic of independent action.

Cluster Synergy

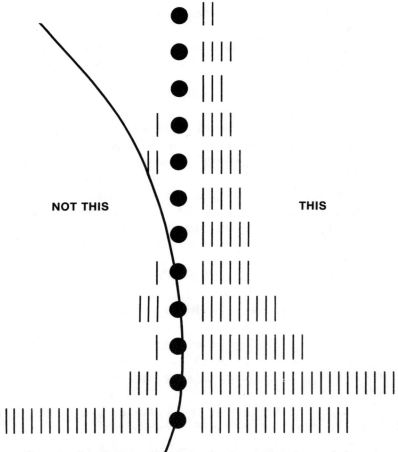

NOT THIS   THIS

There is strength in numbers but only when each truly equals its own value. A small and aggressive retail advertiser in a cluster of stores, whether it be a neighborhood or shopping center, will be better off if each of the other stores would also engage in the practice of advertising their individual wares. Not unlike departments, every specialty store has its sales patterns, selling peaks and ebbs. In a twenty-two store cluster, there is not a month at least two of those stores would have good reason to advertise; their numbers increasing, following the natural sales curve to the Christmas month.

If we agree each store is unique, then we also have to agree each must develop its own strategy to reach its own customer. A unified center effort is no match for a cluster of individual causationists.

It is diffused by committee leadership.

One mind—the strategist's—puts everything in order.

Those of us who believe the problems of today's marketplace are only conditions and variables that need fixing will have a long wait. The fact is our marketing world is indeed different than it was in the 60s. Marketing is like an ocean wave beating the beach. It always remains a wave, but each is different, each comes and goes and is replaced with another. Like it or not, at some time foreign trade will simply have to be expanded. New markets create new customers. When you consider two-thirds of humanity lives in the third world, who can say saturation of goods is complete? Developed countries only recently realized how much they depend on the third world for their supplies. The new entrepreneur has deep convictions a new marketing age is on the horizon. The difference between him and many of us, is that he takes it for granted. *We* believe it is new.

This is how the strategist thinks. The secret to remember is that creativity is a state of mind, and combined with a worldly overview, you will more likely be always consistently better and one step ahead of your competition.

Appendix

ADVERTISING ETHICS AND THE LAW

Our marketing times demand complete integrity. In this new age of sophisticated consumerism, this integrity will put more, not less, impact into your advertisements. This does not mean to imply there ever was a period for anything other than integrity, or that honesty in advertising ever was a negative force.

A successful merchant does not need the FTC to encourage him to police his advertising copy. As an apprentice, one discovers quickly the power of integrity—it's the only way to build a lasting business.

But to advertise with complete integrity is not always an easy undertaking. Though our intentions are good, our time is often limited, and we fail to tell the true and complete selling proposition. In our creative enthusiasm, it is not rare to unintentionally mislead the consumer by omitting pertinent points. The fact remains, our intentions are not suitable excuses for breaking the law . . . and there are laws every advertiser must be well aware of. Four specific areas seem to give retailers the most problems. FTC guides for each are reproduced in this appendix.

1. Deceptive advertising of guarantees
2. Deceptive pricing
3. Bait advertising
4. Warranties

The best advice I received, when I was a young man writing copy for advertisements, was to always put myself in the customer's shoes. You can write better selling copy that way and also be more specific from an honesty point of view. The golden rule applies: do unto others as you would have them do unto you. For example, you cannot kid yourself, manufacturer's list prices are not your regular prices, therefore it is absolutely misleading to quote a savings on this type of comparison. And if you do not intend to sell any reasonable quantity of an advertised item, the advertising intent, we must admit, would be deliberately misleading. There is nothing illegal about stepping up to a similar item with more features, but the advertised item must be on hand if the consumer chooses to stay at that price.

What if a customer buys tires at a reduced price, will the adjustment on the guarantee be applied to your regular price or the sale price the consumer paid? This, we have to admit, is a valid question and deserves explanation in the guarantee or warranty. Guarantees are a particular problem today, because by law, each and all must be totally explained. What you or the manufacturer will actually, factually do must be covered in detail, and in most instances this will require considerable advertising space or media time. The solution, many times, is to drop any reference to guarantees in your advertising, but a manufacturer may demand that it be published. You should never, however, publish any guarantee that does not explain fully exactly what it is, and how the consumer will be satisfied.

The subject of honesty in advertising is a very serious one, and the full responsibility cannot be delegated to a copywriter. Your advertisement is a statement made by your enterprise; that is the way the consumer sees it.

No one can accept the responsibility for guiding another individual to fulfill the integrity requirements to the letter of the law. The responsibility is yours.

It is therefore imperative to note that the FTC clearly states that nothing contained in each of their guides relieves any party subject to the commission's cease and desist order or stipulation. The FTC Guides do not constitute a finding in, and will not affect the disposition of, any formal or informal matter before the commission.

GUIDES, POLICIES, INTERPRETATIONS

[¶ 39,011]   Bait Advertising

16 CFR 238; adopted November 24, 1959.

§ 238.0   Bait advertising defined.[1]

Bait advertising is an alluring but insincere offer to sell a product or service which the advertiser in truth does not intend or want to sell. Its purpose is to switch consumers from buying the advertised merchandise, in order to sell something else, usually at a higher price or on a basis more advantageous to the advertiser. The primary aim of a bait advertisement is to obtain leads as to persons interested in buying merchandise of the type so advertised.

§ 238.1   Bait advertisement.

No advertisement containing an offer to sell a product should be published when the offer is not a bona fide effort to sell the advertised product. (Guide 1.)

§ 238.2   Initial offer.

(a) No statement or illustration should be used in any advertisement which creates a false impression of the grade, quality, make, value, currency of model, size, color, usability, or origin of the product offered, or which may otherwise misrepresent the product in such a manner that later, on disclosure of the true facts, the purchaser may be switched from the advertised product to another.

(b) Even though the true facts are subsequently made known to the buyer, the law is violated if the first contact or interview is secured by deception. (Guide 2.)

§ 238.3   Discouragement of purchase of advertised merchandise.

No act or practice should be engaged in by an advertiser to discourage the purchase of the advertised merchandise as part of a bait scheme to sell other merchandise.

Among acts or practices which will be considered in determining if an advertisement is a bona fide offer are:

(a) The refusal to show, demonstrate, or sell the product offered in accordance with the terms of the offer.

(b) The disparagement by acts or words of the advertised product or the disparagement of the guarantee, credit terms, availability of service, repairs or parts, or in any other respect, in connection with it,

(c) The failure to have available at all outlets listed in the advertisement a sufficient quantity of the advertised product to meet reasonably anticipated demands, unless the advertisement clearly and adequately discloses that supply is limited and/or the merchandise is available only at designated outlets,

(d) The refusal to take orders for the advertised merchandise to be delivered within a reasonable period of time,

(e) The showing or demonstrating of a product which is defective, unusable or impractical for the purpose represented or implied in the advertisement.

---

[1] For the purpose of this part "advertising" includes any form of public notice however disseminated or utilized.

(f) Use of a sales plan or method of compensation for salesman or penalizing salesmen, designed to prevent or discourage them from selling the advertised product. (Guide 3.)

§ 238.4 Switch after sale.

No practice should be pursued by an advertiser, in the event of sale of the advertised product, of "unselling" with the intent and purpose of selling other merchandise in its stead.

Among acts or practices which will be considered in determining if the initial sale was in good faith, and not a strategem to sell other merchandise, are:

(a) Accepting a deposit for the advertised product, then switching the purchaser to a higher-priced product,

(b) Failure to make delivery of the advertised product within a reasonable time or to make a refund,

(c) Disparagement by acts or words of the advertised product, or the disparagement of the guarantee, credit terms, availability of service, repairs, or in any other respect, in connection with it,

(d) The delivery of the advertised product which is defective, unusable or impractical for the purpose represented or implied in the advertisement. (Guide 4.)

● ● ●

NOTE: *Sales of advertised merchandise.*

Sales of the advertised merchandise do not preclude the existence of a bait and switch scheme. It has been determined that, on occasions, this is a mere incidental by-product of the fundamental plan and is intended to provide an aura of legitimacy to the over-all operation.

Nothing contained in these Guides relieves any party subject to a Commission cease and desist order or stipulation from complying with the provisions of such order or stipulation. The Guides do not constitute a finding in and will not affect the disposition of any formal or informal matter before the Commission.

[¶ 39,013]   Deceptive Advertising of Guarantees
16 CFR 239; adopted April 26, 1960.

§ 239.0   Determining violations.

In determining whether terminology and direct or implied representations concerning guarantees, however made, i.e., in advertising or otherwise, in connection with the sale or offering for sale of a product, may be in violation of the Federal Trade Commission Act, the following general principles will be used:

§ 239.1   Guarantees in general.

In general, any guarantee in advertising shall clearly and conspicuously disclose—

(a) *The nature and extent of the guarantee.*

This includes disclosure of—

(1) What product or part of the product is guaranteed,

(2) What characteristics or properties of the designated product or part thereof are covered by, or excluded from, the guarantee,

(3) What is the duration of the guarantee,

(4) What, if anything, any one claiming under the guarantee must do before the guarantor will fulfill his obligation under the guarantee, such as return of the product and payment of service or labor charges; and

(b) *The manner in which the guarantor will perform.*

This consists primarily of a statement of exactly what the guarantor undertakes to do under the guarantee. Examples of this would be repair, replacement, refund. If the guarantor or the person receiving the guarantee has an option as to what may satisfy the guarantee this should be set out; and

(c) *The identity of the guarantor.*

The identity of the guarantor should be clearly revealed in all advertising, as well as in any documents evidencing the guarantee. Confusion of purchasers often occurs when it is not clear whether the manufacturer or the retailer is the guarantor. (Guide 1.)

§ 239.2 Prorata adjustment of guarantees.

(a) Many guarantees are adjusted by the guarantor on a prorata basis. The advertising of these guarantees should clearly disclose this fact, the basis on which they will be prorated, e.g., the time for which the guaranteed product has been used, and the manner in which the guarantor will perform.

(b) If these guarantees are to be adjusted on the basis of a price other than that paid by the purchaser, this price should be clearly and conspicuously disclosed.

Example: "A" sells a tire with list price of $48 to "B" for $24, with a 12 months guarantee. After 6 months use the tire proves defective. If "A" adjusts on the basis of the price "B" paid, $24, "B" will only have to pay one-half of $24, or $12, for a new tire. If "A" instead adjusts on the basis of list price, "B" will owe one-half of $48, or $24, for a new tire. The guarantor would be required to disclose here the following: That this was a 12 months guarantee, that a list price of $48 would be used in the adjustment, that there would be an adjustment on the basis of the time that the tire was used, and that he would not pay the adjusted amount in cash, but would make an adjustment on a new tire.

NOTE: Guarantees which provide for an adjustment based on a fictitious list price should not be used even where adequate disclosure of the price used is made. (Guide 2.)

§ 239.3 "Satisfaction or Your Money Back" representations.

(a) "Satisfaction or Your Money Back," "10 Day Free Trial," or similar representations will be construed as a guarantee that the full purchase price will be refunded at the option of the purchaser.

(b) If this guarantee is subject to any conditions or limitations whatsoever, they shall be set forth as provided for in § 239.1.

Example: A rose bush is advertised under the representation "Satisfaction or Your Money Back." The guarantor requires return of the product within 1 year of purchase date before he will make refund. These limitations, i.e., "return" and "time" shall be clearly and conspicuously disclosed in the ad. (Guide 3.)

§ 239.4 Lifetime guarantees.

If the words "Life," "Lifetime," or the like, are used in advertising to show the duration of a guarantee, and they relate to any life other than that of the purchaser or original user, the life referred to shall be clearly and conspicuously disclosed.

Example: "A" advertised that his carburetor was guaranteed for life, whereas his guarantee ran for the life of the car in which the carburetor was originally installed. The advertisement is ambiguous and deceptive and should be modified to disclose the "life" referred to. (Guide 4.)

§ 239.5 Savings guarantees.

(a) Advertisements frequently contain representations of guarantees that assure prospective purchasers that savings may be realized in the purchase of the advertiser's products.

(b) Some typical advertisements of this type are "Guaranteed to save you 50%," "Guaranteed never to be undersold," "Guaranteed lowest price in town."

(c) These advertisements should include a clear and conspicuous disclosure of what the guarantor will do if the savings are not realized, together with any time or other limitations that he may impose.

Example: "Guaranteed lowest price in town" might be accompanied by the following disclosure:

"If within 30 days from the date that you buy a sewing machine from me, you purchase the identical machine in town for less and present a receipt therefor to me, I will refund your money."

NOTE: The above guarantees may constitute affirmative representations of fact and, in this respect, are governed by § 239.7. (Guide 5.)

§ 239.6 Guarantees under which the guarantor does not or cannot perform.

(a) A seller or manufacturer should not advertise or represent that a product is guaranteed when he cannot or does not promptly and scrupulously fulfill his obligations under the guarantee.

(b) A specific example of refusal to perform obligations under the guarantee is use of "Satisfaction or your money back" when the guarantor cannot or does not intend promptly to make full refund upon request. (Guide 6.)

§ 239.7 Guarantee as a misrepresentation.

Guarantees are often employed in such a manner as to constitute representations of material facts. If such is the case, the guarantor not only undertakes to perform under the terms of the guarantee, but also assumes responsibility under the law for the truth of the representations made.

Example 1: "Guaranteed for 36 months" applied to a battery is a representation that the battery can normally be expected to last for 36 months and should not be used in connection with a battery which can normally be expected to last for only 18 months.

Example 2: "Guaranteed to grow hair or money back" is a representation that the product will grow hair and should not be used when in fact such product is incapable of growing hair.

Example 3: "Guaranteed lowest prices in town" is a representation that the advertiser's prices are lower than the prices charged by all others for the same products in the same town and should not be used when such is not the fact.

Example 4: "We guarantee you will earn $500 a month" is a representation that prospective employees will earn a minimum of $500 each month and should not be used unless such is the fact. (Guide 7.)

Nothing contained in these Guides relieves any party subject to a Commission cease and desist order or stipulation from complying with the provisions of such order or stipulation. The guides do not constitute a finding in and will not affect the disposition of any formal or informal matter before the Commission.

[¶ 39,015]   Deceptive Pricing

16 CFR 233; effective January 8, 1964.

§ 233.1   **Former price comparisons.**

(a) One of the most commonly used forms of bargain advertising is to offer a reduction from the advertiser's own former price for an article. If the former price is the actual, bona fide price at which the article was offered to the public on a regular basis for a reasonably substantial period of time, it provides a legitimate basis for the advertising of a price comparison. Where the former price is genuine, the bargain being advertised is a true one. If, on the other hand, the former price being advertised is not bona fide, but fictitious—for example, where an artificial, inflated price was established for the purpose of enabling the subsequent offer of a large reduction—the "bargain" being advertised is a false one; the purchaser is not receiving the unusual value he expects. In such a case, the "reduced" price is, in reality, probably just the seller's regular price.

(b) A former price is not necessarily fictitious merely because no sales at the advertised price were made. The advertiser should be especially careful, however, in such a case, that the price is one at which the product was openly and actively offered for sale, for a reasonably substantial period of time, in the recent, regular course of his business, honestly and in good faith—and, of course, not for the purpose of establishing a fictitious higher price on which a deceptive comparison might be based. And the advertiser should scrupulously avoid any implication that a former price is a selling, not an asking price (for example, by use of such language as, "formerly sold at $ . . . . . ."), unless substantial sales at that price were actually made.

(c) The following is an example of a price comparison based on a fictitious former price. John Doe is a retailer of Brand X fountain pens, which cost him $5 each. His usual markup is 50 percent over cost; that is, his regular retail price is $7.50. In order subsequently to offer an unusual "bargain," Doe begins offering Brand X at $10 per pen. He realizes that he will be able to sell no, or very few, pens at this inflated price. But he doesn't care, for he maintains that price for only a few days. Then he "cuts" the price to its usual level—$7.50—and advertises: "Terrific Bargain: X Pens, Were $10, Now Only $7.50!" This is obviously a false claim. The advertised "bargain" is not genuine.

(d) Other illustrations of fictitious price comparisons could be given. An advertiser might use a price at which he never offered the article at all; he might feature a price which was not used in the regular course of business, or which was not used in the recent past but at some remote period in the past, without making disclosure of that fact; he might use a price that was not openly offered to the public, or that was not maintained for a reasonable length of time, but was immediately reduced.

(e) If the former price is set forth in the advertisement, whether accompanied or not by descriptive terminology such as "Regularly," "Usually," "Formerly," etc., the advertiser should make certain that the former price is not a fictitious one. If the former price, or the amount or percentage of reduction, is not stated in the advertisement, as when the ad merely states, "Sale," the advertiser must take care that the amount of reduction is not so insignificant as to be meaningless. It should be sufficiently large that the consumer, if he knew what it was, would believe that a genuine bargain or saving was being offered. An advertiser who claims that an item has been "Reduced to $9.99," when the former price was $10, is misleading the consumer, who will understand the claim to mean that a much greater, and not merely nominal, reduction was being offered. [Guide I]

§ 233.2 Retail price comparisons; comparable value comparisons.

(a) Another commonly used form of bargain advertising is to offer goods at prices lower than those being charged by others for the same merchandise in the advertiser's trade area (the area in which he does business). This may be done either on a temporary or a permanent basis, but in either case the advertised higher price must be based upon fact, and not be fictitious or misleading. Whenever an advertiser represents that he is selling below the prices being charged in his area for a particular article, he should be reasonably certain that the higher price he advertises does not appreciably exceed the price at which substantial sales of the article are being made in the area—that is, a sufficient number of sales so that a consumer would consider a reduction from the price to represent a genuine bargain or saving. Expressed another way, if a number of the principal retail outlets in the area are regularly selling Brand X fountain pens at $10, it is not dishonest for retailer Doe to advertise: "Brand X Pens, Price Elsewhere $10, Our Price $7.50."

(b) The following example, however, illustrates a misleading use of this advertising technique. Retailer Doe advertises Brand X pens as having a "Retail Value $15.00, My Price $7.50," when the fact is that only a few small suburban outlets in the area charge $15. All of the larger outlets located in and around the main shopping areas charge $7.50, or slightly more or less. The advertisement here would be deceptive, since the price charged by the small suburban outlets would have no real significance to Doe's customers, to whom the advertisement of "Retail Value $15.00" would suggest a prevailing, and not merely an isolated and unrepresentative, price in the area in which they shop.

(c) A closely related form of bargain advertising is to offer a reduction from the prices being charged either by the advertiser or by others in the advertiser's trade area for other merchandise of like grade and quality—in other words, comparable or competing merchandise—to that being advertised. Such advertising can serve a useful and legitimate purpose when it is made clear to the consumer that a comparison is being made with other merchandise and the other merchandise is, in fact, of essentially similar quality and obtainable in the area. The advertiser should, however, be reasonably certain, just as in the case of comparisons involving the same merchandise, that the price advertised as being the price of comparable merchandise does not exceed the price at which such merchandise is being offered by representative retail outlets in the area. For example, retailer Doe advertises Brand X pen as having "Comparable Value $15.00." Unless a reasonable number of the principal outlets in the area are offering Brand Y, an essentially similar pen, for that price, this advertisement would be deceptive. [Guide II]

§ 233.3 Advertising retail prices which have been established or suggested by manufacturers (or other nonretail distributors).

(a) Many members of the purchasing public believe that a manufacturer's list price, or suggested retail price, is the price at which an article is generally sold. Therefore, if a reduction from this price is advertised, many people will believe that they are being offered a genuine bargain. To the extent that list or suggested retail prices do not in fact correspond to prices at which a substantial number of sales of the article in question are made, the advertisement of a reduction may mislead the consumer.

(b) There are many methods by which manufacturers' suggested retail or list prices are advertised: large scale (often nationwide) mass-media advertising by the manufacturer himself; preticketing by the manufacturer; direct mail advertising; distribution of promotional material or price lists designed for display to the public. The mechanics used are not of the essence. This part is concerned with any means employed for placing such prices before the consuming public.

(c) There would be little problem of deception in this area if all products were invariably sold at the retail price set by the manufacturer. However, the widespread failure to observe manufacturers' suggested or list prices, and the advent of retail discounting on a wide scale, have seriously undermined the dependability of list prices as indicators of the exact prices at which articles are in fact generally sold at retail. Changing competitive conditions have created a more acute problem of deception than may have existed previously. Today, only in the rare case are all sales of an article at the manufacturer's suggested retail or list price.

(d) But this does not mean that all list prices are fictitious and all offers of reductions from list, therefore, deceptive. Typically, a list price is a price at which articles are sold, if not everywhere, then at least in the principal retail outlets which do not conduct their business on a discount basis. It will not be deemed fictitious if it is the price at which substantial (that is, not isolated or insignificant) sales are made in the advertiser's trade area (the area in which he does business). Conversely, if the list price is significantly in excess of the highest price at which substantial sales in the trade area are made, there is a clear and serious danger of the consumer being misled by an advertised reduction from this price.

(e) This general principle applies whether the advertiser is a national or regional manufacturer (or other non-retail distributor), a mail-order or catalog distributor who deals directly with the consuming public, or a local retailer. But certain differences in the responsibility of these various types of businessmen should be noted. A retailer competing in a local area has at least a general knowledge of the prices being charged in his area. Therefore, before advertising a manufacturer's list price as a basis for comparison with his own lower price, the retailer should ascertain whether the list price is in fact the price regularly charged by principal outlets in his area.

(f) In other words, a retailer who advertises a manufacturer's or distributor's suggested retail price should be careful to avoid creating a false impression that he is offering a reduction from the price at which the product is generally sold in his trade area. If a number of the principal retail outlets in the area are regularly engaged in making sales at the manufacturer's suggested price, that price may be used in advertising by one who is selling at a lower price. If, however, the list price is being followed only by, for example, small suburban stores, house-to-house canvassers, and credit houses, accounting for only an insubstantial volume of sales in the area, advertising of the list price would be deceptive.

(g) On the other hand, a manufacturer or other distributor who does business on a large regional or national scale cannot be required to police or investigate in detail the prevailing prices of his articles throughout so large a trade area. If he advertises or disseminates a list or pre-ticketed price in good faith (i.e., as an honest estimate of the actual retail price) which does not appreciably exceed the highest price at which substantial sales are made in his trade area, he will not be chargeable with having engaged in a deceptive practice. Consider the following example:

(h) Manufacturer Roe, who makes Brand X pens and sells them throughout the United States, advertises his pen in a national magazine as having a "Suggested Retail Price $10," a price determined on the basis of a market survey. In a substantial number of representative communities, the principal retail outlets are selling the product at this price in the regular course of business and in substantial volume. Roe would not be considered to have advertised a fictitious "suggested retail price." If retailer Doe does business in one of these communities, he would not be guilty of a deceptive practice by advertising, "Brand X Pens, Manufacturer's Suggested Retail Price, $10, Our Price, $7.50."

(i) It bears repeating that the manufacturer, distributor or retailer must in every case act honestly and in good faith in advertising a list price, and not with the intention of establishing a basis, or creating an instrumentality, for a deceptive comparison in any local or other trade area. For instance, a manufacturer may not affix price tickets containing inflated prices as an accommodation to particular retailers who intend to use such prices as the basis for advertising fictitious price reductions. [Guide III]

§ 233.4 Bargain offers based upon the purchase of other merchandise.

(a) Frequently, advertisers choose to offer bargains in the form of additional merchandise to be given a customer on the condition that he purchase a particular article at the price usually offered by the advertiser. The forms which such offers may take are numerous and varied, yet all have essentially the same purpose and effect. Representative of the language frequently employed in such offers are "Free," "Buy One—Get One Free," "2-For-1 Sale," "Half Price Sale," "1¢ Sale," "50% Off," etc. Literally, of course, the seller is not offering anything "free" (i.e., an unconditional gift), or ½ free, or for only 1¢, when he makes such an offer, since the purchaser is required to purchase an article in order to receive the "free" or "1¢" item. It is important, therefore, that where such a form of offer is used, care be taken not to mislead the consumer.

(b) Where the seller, in making such an offer, increases his regular price of the article required to be bought, or decreases the quantity and quality of that article, or otherwise attaches strings (other than the basic condition that the article be purchased in order for the purchaser to be entitled to the "free" or "1¢" additional merchandise) to the offer, the consumer may be deceived.

(c) Accordingly, whenever a "free," "2-for-1," "half price sale," "1¢ sale," "50% off" or similar type of offer is made, all the terms and conditions of the offer should be made clear at the outset. [Guide IV]

§ 233.5 Miscellaneous price comparisons.

The practices covered in the provisions set forth above represent the most frequently employed forms of bargain advertising. However, there are many variations which appear from time to time and which are, in the main, controlled by the same general principles. For example, retailers should not advertise a retail price as a "wholesale" price. They should not represent that they are selling at "factory" prices when they are not selling at the prices paid by those purchasing directly from the manufacturer. They should not offer seconds or imperfect or irregular merchandise at a reduced price without disclosing that the higher comparative price refers to the price of the merchandise if perfect. They should not offer an advance sale under circumstances where they do not in good faith expect to increase the price at a later date, or make a "limited" offer which, in fact, is not limited. In all of these situations, as well as in others too numerous to mention, advertisers should make certain that the bargain offer is genuine and truthful. Doing so will serve their own interest as well as that of the public. [Guide V]

(Secs. 5, 6, 38 Stat. 719, as amended, 721; 15 U. S. C. 45, 46)

These guides supersede the guides against deceptive pricing adopted October 2, 1958.

These guides have been reproduced with permission from *Trade Regulation Reports*, published and copyrighted by Commerce Clearing House, Inc., Chicago, Ill.

Bibliography

Mortimer J. Adler, *How to Read a Book*. New York: Simon & Schuster/Clarion Book, 1940.

——, *The Time of Our Lives*. New York: Holt, Rinehart and Winston, 1970.

Stafford Beer, *Management Science*. New York: Doubleday & Company, 1967.

Peter F. Drucker, *Management*. New York: Harper & Row, 1974.

Editors of Pensee, *Velikovsky Reconsidered*. New York: Warner Books, 1976.

Richard J. Gentile, *Retail Advertising*. New York: Chain Store Age, 1976.

James L. Heskett, *Marketing*. New York: Macmillan Publishing Co., 1976.

Otto Kleppner, *Advertising Procedure*, 6th ed. Englewood Cliffs, N.J.: Prentice-Hall, 1974.

Walter Lippmann, "Education vs. Western Civilization," *The American Scholar*, 1941.

Malcolm, P. McNair and Eleanor G. May, *The American Department Store 1920-1960*. Boston: Harvard Business School, 1963.

Rosser Reeves, *Reality in Advertising*, New York: Alfred A. Knopf, 1961.

Survey of Current Business. Washington, D.C.: U.S. Department of Commerce, 1972.

Charles Tavel, *The Third Industrial Age—Strategy for Business Survival*. New York: Dow Jones-Irwin, 1975.

Twenty-seventh Annual Timetable of Retail Opportunities. New York: Newspaper Advertising Bureau, 1977.

Immanuel Velikovsky, *Worlds in Collision*. New York: Doubleday & Company, 1950.